# What
# Houseplant
# Where

# What Houseplant Where

## ROY LANCASTER
### *and* MATTHEW BIGGS

**DORLING KINDERSLEY**
London • New York • Sydney • Moscow

## A DORLING KINDERSLEY BOOK

EDITOR Clare Double
ART EDITORS Stuart Perry, Helen Robson
MANAGING EDITOR Jonathan Metcalf
MANAGING ART EDITORS Peter Cross, Steve Knowlden
PRODUCTION MANAGER Michelle Thomas
DTP DESIGNER Robert Campbell

First published in Great Britain in 1998
by Dorling Kindersley Limited, 9 Henrietta Street, London WC2 8PS
Visit us on the World Wide Web at http://www.dk.com

2 4 6 8 10 9 7 5 3 1

A CIP catalogue record for this book is available from the British Library

ISBN 0–7513–0592–8

Text film output by The Right Type, Great Britain
Reproduced by Colorlito, Italy
Printed and bound by Butler and Tanner, Great Britain

# CONTENTS

# How This Book Works

I N THIS BOOK, our aim is both to introduce beginners to the world of houseplants and to alert committed enthusiasts to some of the new plants now available for growing at home. The book is divided into five sections: Floral Effect, Foliage Effect, Locations, Specific Uses, and Specialist Plants. In each,

we have directed readers to a selection of plants that are well suited to a given situation or purpose, or that offer specific ornamental effects through their colour or shape. Brief details of cultivation requirements are also provided to help you achieve long-term success with your houseplants.

### WHAT IS A HOUSEPLANT?

In the broadest sense, a houseplant is any plant grown indoors. Many perfectly hardy garden plants are used for this purpose, but the overwhelming majority of houseplants popular in cool temperate regions are those plants from warmer climates that require heat or high humidity or both in order to thrive. Houseplants are grown for the decorative effects of their flowers, foliage, fruits, or growth habit (shape). They also have therapeutic value: research shows that they clean the air and are beneficial to our health and well-being.

### USING THE CULTIVATION NOTES

Concise notes on the most important care factors are introduced by the following five symbols. See also pages 14–21.

☼ *Light*
Light needs are divided into three categories – Bright, Moderate, and Shady. "Shady" does not mean devoid of light. "Summer sun" means scorching midday sun.

▤ *Temperature and humidity*
Temperatures are given as Low (4–9°C/39–48°F), Moderate (10–15°C/50–59°F), or Warm (16–21°C/61–70°F). Humidity is Low, Moderate, or High.

● *Feeding*
Feed at the specified intervals, when a plant is in active growth (usually spring to autumn). Unless stated in the entry, feed with any general houseplant fertilizer.

◊ *Watering*
References such as "when dry" relate to the compost surface. Water when the stated conditions apply. "Sparingly" means just enough to avoid desiccation.

▨ *Propagation*
The most common and reliable ways of increasing your plants are given in each individual entry. See pages 20–21 for a more detailed explanation of each method.

BOTANICAL •
AND COMMON
PLANT NAMES
*Below each plant's botanical name is the common name or, if none exists, the generic name or group name.*

AGM ♗ •
*The trophy symbol identifies those plants that have received the RHS Award of Garden Merit.*

## Houseplants for Architectural Effect

N O PLANTS CONTRIBUTE more drama to the visual scheme of a room than those with large or deeply divided leaves or a striking habit. Careful siting is important if a plant's architectural qualities are to become a focal point. As a general rule, the bigger the plant and the space around it, the more effective its scale and form will appear.

*Araucaria heterophylla* ▷
NORFOLK ISLAND PINE
‡ 2.5m (8ft) or more ↔ 1.2m (4ft) or more

Like so many houseplants, this reaches a large size in its natural environment. Best grown indoors on a single stem, it is then less vigorous but still impressive. ♗

☼ Bright, but avoid summer sun ▤ Moderate. Moderate humidity ● Fortnightly. Occasionally in winter ◊ When compost surface dry. Water sparingly in winter ▨ Seed

SPECIFIC USES

△ *Beaucarnea recurvata*
ELEPHANT'S FOOT, PONY TAIL
‡ 1.8m (6ft) or more ↔ 1m (3ft) or more

An extraordinary-looking plant from Mexico that develops a bulbous base and a great tonk not of slender, arching or pendulous leaves. Easy to grow.

☼ Bright, with sun ▤ Moderate to warm. Low humidity ● Monthly, using fertilizer for cacti and succulents. ◊ When compost surface dry. Water sparingly in winter ▨ Tip cuttings, offsets, seed

△ *Cycas revoluta*
SAGO PALM
‡ ↔ 1.5m (5ft)

This primitive evergreen, not a true palm, develops its short trunk very slowly, but the stiff, leathery, deeply divided leaves are spectacular even on a young plant. ♗

☼ Bright, but avoid direct summer sun ▤ Warm. Moderate to high humidity ● Monthly ◊ Water when compost surface dry ▨ Seed, buds from old or dormant plants

△ *Dracaena fragrans* 'White Stripe'
DRACAENA
‡ 2m (6ft) or more ↔ 1m (3ft)

A striking foliage plant producing stiffly erect stems and generous clusters of long, pointed green leaves, with white-striped margins. This is a bold specimen plant.

☼ Bright to moderate, avoiding summer sun ▤ Warm. Moderate to high humidity ● Fortnightly. Occasionally in winter ◊ When dry. Water sparingly in winter ▨ Tip cuttings, stem sections

### OTHER NARROW-LEAVED ARCHITECTURAL HOUSEPLANTS

*Cordyline australis*
*Dracaena draco*
*Pandanus veitchii*, see p.43
*Phormium tenax*
*Sansevieria trifasciata*, see p.89
*Yucca elephantipes*, see p.87

96

### OTHER PLANT SUGGESTIONS

The plants featured for each location, purpose, or effect are simply our personal selection of the best available; for many of the categories covered in the book, there is an almost unlimited choice of plants. Boxes on each spread therefore list additional names of other houseplants that are worth considering for the same use. Cross-references are given when the additional suggestions are featured in other categories elsewhere in the book.

OTHER PLANTS •
*These boxes list more plants suitable for the location or that offer the same effect.*

## PLANTS WITH A SEAL OF APPROVAL

The Royal Horticultural Society gives an Award of Garden Merit to plants whose decorative effect, constitution, ease of cultivation, and availability is excellent. It is a useful guide to some of the best plants, but many superb house-plants are not yet so recognized.

♈ *Award of Garden Merit*

## PLANT DIMENSIONS

Dimensions refer to a mature plant's average size when grown indoors. Many are larger in the wild or if unpruned. Height includes flower stems, where appropriate.

↕ *Average height*

↔ *Average spread*

↕↔ *Average height and spread*

## FLORAL EFFECT

Flowers, in their varied shapes and colours, can bring character to a room. Flowering plants are available in many forms, from temporary "pot plants" to those with long-lasting flowers or with blooms produced season after season. This section suggests plants for *Fragrant, Long-lasting, Bold-coloured, Winter or spring,* or *Summer flowers,* or with both *Flowers and foliage.*

## FOLIAGE EFFECT

Foliage can be just as dramatic as flowers, and is longer-lasting. This section identifies plants with a variety of colour effects: *Red, pink, or purple, Gold- or yellow-variegated, White- or cream-variegated,* or *Silver or grey.* Different foliage types, suitable for all kinds of arrangements, are included: *Small, Large, Narrow or sword-shaped, Textured, Aromatic,* and *Unusual foliage.*

## LOCATIONS

Every room has different levels of light, heat, and humidity, and it is important to choose plants to suit these conditions. In this section are suggestions for *Sunny windowsills; Full, Medium,* and *Low light; Dry atmospheres;* and *Warm, humid rooms.* In addition, *Large rooms, Sitting and dining rooms, Bedrooms, Narrow spaces, Garden rooms,* and the *Home office* are all considered.

## SPECIFIC USES

Houseplants are extremely versatile. The huge variety of form, foliage, flowers, and fruits provides an array of suggestions for many specific purposes: *Trailing, Climbing, Architectural effect, Ornamental fruit,* and *Terraria.* For practical uses we suggest *Houseplants for Beginners,* plants *Tolerant of neglect, Beneficial houseplants, Dual-purpose houseplants,* and *Herbs for the kitchen.*

## SPECIALIST PLANTS

The world of houseplants provides wide potential for special interest, with groups that appeal to the collector in all of us. Some are fascinating because they are exceptionally beautiful, some are challenging to cultivate, and others display curious attributes or unusual growth habits. In this section, we offer selections of *Ferns, Cacti and succulents, Orchids, Palms,* and *Bromeliads* for special interest, and *Novelty houseplants.*

**OTHER BROAD-LEAVED ARCHITECTURAL HOUSEPLANTS**

*Chamaedorea elegans,* see p.114
*Howea belmoreana,* see p.115
*Monstera deliciosa,* see p.41
*Pisonia umbellifera*
'Variegata'
*Polyscias fruticosa*
*Radermachera sinica*
*Rhapis excelsa,* see p.115

HOUSEPLANTS FOR ARCHITECTURAL EFFECT

*Dracaena marginata* ▷
**MADAGASCAR DRAGON TREE**
↕ 3m (10ft) ↔ 1.2m (4ft)
Bold tufts of shining, grassy, red-edged green leaves bring a touch of the exotic to any room. This native of Madagascar is one of the most popular dracaenas for indoor cultivation.
Bright to moderate, avoiding summer sun. Warm. Moderate to high humidity. Fortnightly. Occasionally in winter. When dry. Sparingly in winter. Tip cuttings, stem sections

*Schefflera arboricola* 'Gold Capella' ▷
**SCHEFFLERA**
↕ 1.8m (6ft) ↔ 1m (3ft)
The umbrella tree is grown as a house-plant for its long-stalked juvenile foliage, which is divided into rich green, gold-splashed leaflets. A dark background or group setting is effective. ♈
Bright to moderate. Warm, avoiding fluctuation. Moderate to high humidity. Fortnightly. Monthly in winter. Water when compost surface dry. Tip cuttings, air layering

*Large, feather-shaped fronds*

△ *Ficus lyrata*
**BANJO FIG, FIDDLE-LEAF FIG**
↕ 3m (10ft) or more ↔ 1.8m (6ft) or more
Give this plant plenty of elbow room to accommodate its likely spread and show off its spectacular large, waisted leaves. This fig originates in African forests. ♈
Bright. Avoid summer sun. Warm. Moderate to high humidity. Fortnightly. Occasionally in winter. When compost surface dry. Reduce at lower temperatures. Tip cuttings, air layering

△ *Lytocaryum weddellianum*
**DWARF COCONUT PALM**
↕ 2m (6ft) ↔ 1.5m (5ft)
One of the most beautiful palms for the home and tolerant of low light. Handle the fragile roots with care when repotting. Formerly sold as *Microcoelum* or *Cocos*. ♈
Moderate to shady. Warm. Moderate to high humidity. Every three weeks. When compost surface dry. Water sparingly in winter. Avoid waterlogging. Seed

△ *Schefflera elegantissima* 'Castor'
**FALSE ARALIA, FINGER ARALIA**
↕ 2m (6ft) ↔ 90cm (3ft)
This plant produces an elegant, lacy outline. The dark coppery-green leaves have long, narrow leaflets that widen with age. Also known as *Aralia* or *Dizygotheca*.
Bright, avoiding direct sun. Warm, avoiding fluctuation. Moderate humidity. Fortnightly. Monthly at low winter temperatures. Water when dry. Avoid overwatering. Tip cuttings, seed

• HEIGHT AND SPREAD
*Measurements indicate the average size of the plant when grown indoors, in metric and imperial.*

• THUMB MARKER
*These identify each of the five sections in the book (see right).*

• PLANT PROFILE
*Concise text describes the main decorative features and special uses of each plant.*

97

• CULTIVATION NOTES
*Symbols introduce brief details of light, temperature, humidity, feeding, and watering requirements, plus propagation methods.*

## PLANT NAMES

Currently accepted botanical species and cultivar names are used in this book. Where we show one of many similar hybrids the name is general, such as "*Cattleya* hybrids", rather than specific. Common names in current use are given; where none exists, the generic name is repeated, or an English name common to the whole genus or group (such as "scented geranium") is used. All names are indexed.

**FLORAL EFFECT**

**FOLIAGE EFFECT**

**LOCATIONS**

**SPECIFIC USES**

**SPECIALIST PLANTS**

# INTRODUCTION

ANYONE WHO HAS SUCCESSFULLY grown plants at home will know the satisfaction of cultivating healthy and attractive houseplants. They offer many different ornamental effects and bring the natural world indoors – a particularly welcome feature in homes without gardens.

△ URBAN JUNGLE *Houseplants bring nature into your home. This collection of bromeliads softens the harsh city view.*

Many people are discouraged from growing houseplants by an initial lack of success. In this book, we not only offer advice on caring for each plant, but on where to site it. This is a crucial part of successful cultivation, and a plant's native origins (see pages 10–11) can provide some valuable clues to the kind of indoor environment in which it will thrive. We aim to guarantee good results every time by suggesting the most suitable plants for the different areas of the home, finding the best plant for each mini-environment – whether it is a warm, humid room or a low-light corner.

Choosing the right plant for the right place is just one important part of growing houseplants well. Once settled, they need regular care if they are to flourish – a little time spent each day on watering and feeding may be all that is required. A guide to houseplant care can be found on pages 14–21.

## DECORATING WITH PLANTS

Just as a gardener uses the shapes and colours of different plants to create a look or theme in the garden, you can "decorate" your home with houseplants. They can complement the colour or texture of the furniture or the decorative style of a room. Beyond that, they provide a visual link between one room and the next, and with the garden or street outside. We offer houseplants for the ornamental effects of their flowers and foliage, and for specific uses, such as plants that climb or those with an architectural habit. Suggestions are included to enable you to make the most of flowers throughout the seasons.

## HOUSEPLANTS FOR HEALTH

Most houseplants are superbly ornamental, but research has shown that they also absorb many of the airborne pollutants released by cleaning products, materials used in building, and new furnishings – and of course they add oxygen and moisture to the air that we breathe indoors. Houseplants really do make for a healthier home environment. In addition, the everyday routine of houseplant maintenance – picking off a dead leaf or faded flower, spraying with cool water, and general care and attention – is soothing and satisfying, and can even reduce feelings of stress.

## BEGINNER OR EXPERT

Rest assured that you do not need to be a skilled indoor gardener to grow houseplants – many are easy for beginners to cultivate, giving novices the confidence to become more adventurous. Also featured in this book are selections of special plant groups, such as orchids, ferns, and bromeliads, each with their own characteristics. These may appeal to collectors or inspire you to grow something a little different.

◁ FORMAL DISPLAY *This carefully arranged display of plain and variegated green foliage plants focuses on their leaf textures and shapes for its effect.*

## AUTHORS' CHOICES

We cannot, in a single book, hope to answer every question about houseplants. What we can do is pass on our enthusiasm and affinity for these plants, which, combined with our training and experience of them in the wild, has inspired us to put together this collection. Like the other titles in this series, *What Houseplant Where* helps you choose the right plants for each location in your home. The plants featured are not, of course, all that are available, but simply our choice of the best that we have grown, or admired in the homes of others.

▷ MODERN SIMPLICITY *There is a houseplant to complement every style of interior design. This architectural plant is well suited to an uncluttered setting.*

▽ RICH CHOICE *This group, containing bright colours and green shades, bold leaves and delicate flowers, hints at the great variety in the houseplant world.*

# Where do Houseplants Come From?

I F WE WERE TO REPRODUCE at home the environments in which many houseplants grow in the wild, we would have to move out – the conditions in which most of them grow would be very oppressive to us. But knowledge of a plant's native habitat can help you understand and meet at least some of its needs, giving it the best opportunity to flourish in your home. The majority of plants that can be grown indoors come from one of three main climate types: tropical, semi-desert, and Mediterranean.

### TROPICAL RAINFOREST
Tropical rainforests are mainly found in south-east Asia, north-east Australia, equatorial Africa, and Central and South America. Here, constant warmth, high humidity,

◁ RAINFOREST CLIMBER *Canopy dwellers such as this* Philodendron erubescens *'Red Emerald' require medium light and high humidity to thrive – conditions similar to those in their rainforest homes.*

and plentiful rainfall combine to encourage lush, continuous, varied plant growth. Vines and creepers such as *Epipremnum*, *Monstera*, and *Philodendron* climb into the canopy of tall trees, so at home they need plenty of space and the support of a moist moss pole or frame. The trees' often moss-clad branches are home to many epiphytes – non-parasitic plants that prefer to live above the competition on the forest floor. Epiphytes commonly grown as houseplants include many ferns and orchids, and most bromeliads, including *Aechmea*, *Billbergia*, *Tillandsia*, and *Vriesea*. You can grow epiphytes on bark or in hanging baskets made for indoor use. The tropical rainforest's dim, decaying floor, protected from the sun's glare by the canopy, is the natural habitat of foliage plants like *Aglaonema*, *Anthurium*, *Calathea*, *Dieffenbachia*, and *Syngonium*. In the home, they need a warm humid atmosphere away from direct sun.

### ARID OR SEMI-DESERT
Semi-desert habitats are found in parts of southern Africa, the south-west United States, Mexico, and South America. These dry, sunny regions, which can be scorching by day and freezing cold at night, are home to a surprising number of plants, including *Aloe*, *Crassula*, *Euphorbia*, *Haworthia*, *Kalanchoe*, and cacti like *Echinocactus*, *Ferocactus*, *Mammillaria*, *Opuntia*, *Oreocereus*, and *Rebutia*. Many cacti and succulents that enjoy hot, dry conditions are best suited to sunny windowsills or similar spots in the house. However, epiphytic cacti, such as *Rhipsalis* and *Schlumbergera* from Brazil and *Epiphyllum* from Mexico and Central America to the

◁ PUERTO RICAN RAINFOREST *The lush vegetation covers every inch of space as plants compete for light and moisture. The tree hosts an epiphytic bromeliad.*

◁ SEMI-DESERT CLIMATE *Arid regions, like this Arizona canyon, are home to a surprising array of species.* Oreocereus trollii, *left, is a typical dry heat lover.*

## NATURAL LIGHT

For the majority of flowering plants, from seasonal plants like *Cyclamen* to exotics such as *Bougainvillea*, good light is the most crucial factor, whatever their origin or heat and humidity requirements. There are also many flowering plants from cool temperate European areas, such as snowdrops and primroses, that are hardy and can be planted in the garden after flowering.

## ADAPTABLE SURVIVORS

Remember, plants are extremely adaptable, hence their survival in many challenging habitats. Don't be put off trying to grow them at home; they can tolerate seemingly adverse conditions so long as these are not severe or permanent.

West Indies, are forest dwellers, and therefore cannot tolerate exposure to the hottest summer sun.

## TEMPERATE MEDITERRANEAN

In between these two extremes are regions that enjoy a Mediterranean climate of warm, usually dry summers and mild, often wet winters. The Mediterranean basin, South Africa, south-east Australia, parts of the south-west United States, and central Chile are such areas. Many houseplants, including *Boronia*, Cape heaths, *Euryops, Myrtus, Pelargonium, Prostanthera, Strelitzia*, and many palms, originate in this type of climate. Indoors, a warm, sunny spot and regular watering are ideal conditions for most of them.

▷ MEDITERRANEAN PALMS *The Canary Island date palm (*Phoenix canariensis*), right, and the Chilean wine palm (*Jubaea chilensis*), far right, can both be grown indoors when young.*

# Choosing the Right Plants for your Home

T HE RIGHT PLANT in the right location will be healthy, full of vitality, and will flourish for years; an unsuitable plant in the wrong place will never perform well, and may even die. So take time to match a houseplant to the conditions in the spot you wish to fill, and consider other factors, such as tolerance of neglect, that may also affect where you place it.

△ BEDROOMS *In your own room, let personal taste dominate – here, bold foliage makes a statement. Temperatures are usually moderate and rarely fluctuate, which is ideal for many plants.*

Foliage begonias for the sitting room

*Low-light position* Cool, shady spots are ideal for ivies or aspidistras.

*Seasonal plant* Easy to care for, seasonal plants often provide a splash of colour.

*Uncluttered corner* Large leaves are easy to reach for cleaning.

BEDROOM

SITTING ROOM

*Specimen plant* A bold or coloured foliage plant makes an impact in a medium-lit spot.

*Medium light* This semi-screened window will suit many foliage plants.

*Dry atmosphere* Grow bromeliads or any other plants that tolerate dry air above a radiator in winter.

*Table display* Low-growing plants do n[ot] interrupt the view across the room.

*Small feature* This bright begonia sets off the pale furnishings.

## LIGHT DISTRIBUTION

*Low light* is tolerated by a limited number of plants

*Shady areas* are suitable for temporary displays only

*Moderate light* near the window suits a wide range of plants

*Full light* Windowsills in full sun offer most light, but this is too strong for many plants

▷ SITTING AND DINING ROOMS *A bold group of plants assembled in the corner of a sitting or dining room creates a wonderful indoor "border". Place them carefully with taller plants at the back, choosing their colours to complement or contrast with the decorative scheme.*

## COMMON HAZARDS

Handle poisonous plants with care, and teach children not to eat any plant material or compost. Site poisonous or spiny plants out of reach, and leave walkways clear of hanging baskets or large, floor-standing plants. Attach hanging baskets and brackets securely.

▷ BATHROOMS *A light, warm bathroom, the ideal home for exotic houseplants, is a good place in which to create your own miniature "jungle". Regular showers create humidity, but beware of open windows letting in chilly draughts.*

*High humidity* Ferns thrive in warm, humid, medium-lit spots like the corner of this bath.

*Neglected corner* Plants tucked away in corners may be overlooked; yuccas tolerate neglect.

*Exotic specimen* This stromanthe, like other exotics, can flourish in a warm bathroom.

BATHROOM

LANDING

## PROBLEM CORNERS

All plants need some light; few will be happy in dark corners. Use temporary houseplants here, or permanent ones for a few weeks only. Reflect light into the area with mirrors, or paint the surrounding walls white. An aspidistra is one of the few plants that tolerates draughty corners opposite doors.

*Draughty hallway* The front door brings in cold draughts that may kill plants.

HOME OFFICE

*Clean air* Use beneficial plants to help counteract emissions from office equipment.

HALL

*Heat lover* An *Aloe vera* will withstand being near the oven and its leaves can soothe burns.

*Holiday watering* Group plants on capillary matting in a cool spot when you are away.

*Living colour* Use a saintpaulia or other flowering plant to decorate the table.

KITCHEN

Mixed herbs for the kitchen

*Sunny windowsill* This is the ideal location for a selection of herbs.

*Windowsill without direct sun* Perfect for cuttings. A frequently visited location is also good for a plant "hospital".

◁ KITCHENS *Fluctuating heat and humidity and draughts can be problems here. Position plants in corners, on windowsills, and on surfaces away from work areas. Consider raising cuttings in the kitchen, as you will see them every day.*

## DESIGNING WITH HOUSEPLANTS

When buying plants, take carpet or paint samples from your room so you can choose a plant that complements or contrasts with the decor. Consider the shape of the plant and its leaves, its overall size, the space you have available, and also how large it will be when mature – many plants on sale are juvenile. If you can't find exactly what you want, remember that a plain green-leaved plant suits any setting.

# Everyday Care

GOOD HUSBANDRY is necessary if you want to grow quality houseplants that are noticed for the right reasons. Having chosen a healthy plant, and found a position that satisfies its needs for light and heat, a regular feeding and watering routine is essential. It may take a little time each day, but the effort will be handsomely rewarded.

## SELECTING A HEALTHY SPECIMEN

Buy plants from reputable outlets such as florists or garden centres, rather than from grocery stores or garages where they are often an afterthought. Look around to find a good quality supplier. Avoid buying tender plants, like poinsettias, if they have been displayed on a cold pavement or in a draughty shop.

CHECK FOR PESTS
*Look for pests under the leaves and on any flower buds and growing tips.*

CHECK FOR STEM ROT
*Inspect the centre for any slimy or rotting leaves.*

Before you buy, give the plant a quick health check. It should be undamaged, have a good shape, and its leaves should show no signs of wilting. Check for signs of pests or diseases (see left). Flowering plants should have many buds, a few open flowers, and no dead blooms. Bulbs should be plump and undamaged. A plant's roots are also a good indicator of its health – don't be afraid to knock a plant from the pot for a closer look. Ignore any plant with a sparse or poor-looking root system, or one whose pot is congested with roots – a sure sign is if roots are growing through the pot's drainage holes. Ensure the compost is moist, neither bone dry nor waterlogged. Finally, avoid plants with signs of "display fatigue" – tired-looking, lacklustre specimens.

### TRANSPORTING PURCHASES

Protect plants on the journey home in a bag, box, or plastic sleeve. Stand and secure new purchases on a level surface to prevent them from falling over and being damaged. Tender plants are very vulnerable in cold weather, so a warm car is excellent for transporting them in autumn and winter. But don't leave any plant in a hot car for long, as it will soon dry out and wilt.

USE A PROTECTIVE PLASTIC SLEEVE

### ACCLIMATIZING NEW PLANTS

When you arrive home, unwrap your new plant immediately and water it if necessary. Find a position which suits most of the plant's needs, and allow two or three weeks for it to settle in. Plants may initially shed flowers or leaves in shock, but if you keep on providing the correct care, they should recover quickly. Try not to move plants until they are acclimatized.

GIVE NEW PLANTS TIME TO SETTLE IN

## LIGHT

Most houseplants thrive in moderate to bright light, and the nearer you can get to satisfying each plant's individual needs, the better it will grow. Note that plants with variegated or coloured leaves usually need higher light levels than green-leaved plants.

Only a few plant groups, like cacti and succulents, can tolerate scorching sun, which can be particularly fierce when it is magnified by the glass of a window. Always provide protection or relief from the hottest summer sun, even for sun-loving plants. Shade-tolerant plants, particularly those with brightly coloured leaves, can be used for temporary display in very dark corners, but remember to move them into a brighter position every two or three weeks to recover. You can also use "grow lamps" or fluorescent tubes to provide light in these conditions and where winter light levels are extremely low.

As plants naturally grow towards the nearest light source, turn their pots regularly to encourage balanced growth. The exceptions are some flowering plants, such as *Schlumbergera*, as turning causes their buds to drop.

SUN-SEEKER
*This plant has grown bent over in the direction of a light source.*

## TEMPERATURE

If the temperature is too low for a plant, its growth slows or stops; too high and its growth is spindly, particularly at low light levels. However, plants will often tolerate lower temperatures (for example in winter) if watering is reduced. Equally, with notable exceptions like cacti and succulents, most plants will tolerate higher temperatures provided humidity is increased and ventilation improved. However, most houseplants prefer a constant temperature; beware of draughts, radiators being switched off at night, or the use of cookers and other household equipment, which can cause heat levels to fluctuate. In addition, when overnight temperatures are low, move plants from windowsills before closing the curtains, as even central heating will not protect plants from the sharp drop in temperature. Otherwise, leave curtains open.

## HUMIDITY

MOIST PEBBLE TRAY
*Stand pots on a layer of pebbles. Add water to just below the base of the pots, topping up when necessary.*

As a general rule, the higher the temperature, the higher the humidity plants will need. One easy way of increasing humidity is to mist your plants with an atomizer several times a day. Use tepid soft water; in hard-water areas, use cooled boiled water or fresh rainwater, or you may find chalky deposits on the leaves. Do not spray delicate blooms, particularly in bright light, or hairy-leaved plants, and avoid spraying the surrounding furnishings. Alternatively, group plants with similar requirements together, preferably on a pebble tray (see above). Each plant will transpire moisture, increasing humidity. You can also stand a plant inside a larger pot or container, fill the space between the two with moist peat substitute, and water as needed. Enthusiasts might buy a humidifier.

## FEEDING

Regular feeding is essential for good results. Use flowering houseplant (or tomato) fertilizer to promote flowering, and foliage houseplant fertilizer (high in nitrogen) for leaf growth. Otherwise, use general fertilizer, which contains balanced nutrients for healthy growth. Where fertilizer for ericaceous plants is recommended, that plant will also benefit from soft water and lime-free compost. Feed only during active growth; unless stated in the individual entry, do not feed a resting plant. Never feed a plant if its compost is dry or waterlogged. Underfeeding makes plants weak and lacklustre; overfeeding causes the roots to scorch and produces symptoms similar to those of overwatering.

FOLIAR FEEDING
*Misting with dilute liquid fertilizer boosts flagging plants.*

Slow-release fertilizers, in the form of spikes or pills (see below), are added to the compost and are ideal if you are likely to forget to feed your plants; liquid fertilizer or soluble powder types are rapidly absorbed. Special fertilizers are produced for specific plant groups such as African violets, cacti, ericaceous plants, and orchids.

### FERTILIZER TYPES

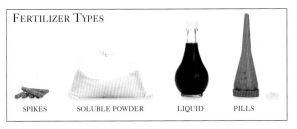

SPIKES     SOLUBLE POWDER     LIQUID     PILLS

## WATERING

Water with care – overwatering kills more houseplants than anything else, but give too little water and the roots at the bottom of the pot will desiccate. To judge if a plant needs watering, push your finger into the compost; if soil adheres, it is still moist. Alternatively, squeeze some soil between your fingers to check how moist it is, or use water indicator sticks that change colour when water is needed.

WATER FROM BELOW
*Fill the saucer with water; discard any not absorbed.*

Always use tepid water. Tap water is fine for most plants, except in hard-water areas, where cooled boiled tap water, or fresh rainwater, should be used. Acid-loving plants like azaleas always need soft water. Plants in small pots, those with hairy leaves, and cyclamen should be watered from below (see left). Otherwise, topwatering (see below), using a watering can with a narrow spout, suits most plants. After watering, drain any excess away; do not allow the pot to stand in a saucer of water. Plants that have been allowed to dry out should be immersed in water (see below). Remove waterlogged plants from the pot and allow compost to dry before repotting.

TOPWATERING
*Water the compost, avoiding the leaves.*

REVIVING A PARCHED PLANT
*Break up dry soil, then stand the pot in a bowl of tepid water until moist; spray the leaves. Drain, and allow to recover.*

### CLEANING HOUSEPLANTS

Wipe glossy leaves (right) with a soft, slightly damp cloth or cotton wool. If they are very dusty, use a soft brush first. Do not dust or wipe new leaves, as they are easily damaged. "Leaf shine" can be used occasionally on smooth leaves but not on young or hairy leaves. Dust hairy leaves with a make-up brush (left). To wash plants, stand them out in light, warm spring or summer rain, or under a tepid, soft-water shower at low pressure. Invert small plants into a bowl of tepid water. Wrap the pot in a plastic bag, or use your fingers, to stop the compost falling out.

# Longer-term Maintenance

ALONGSIDE THE daily routine of house-plant care, other tasks are necessary to ensure that your plants remain in excellent condition. Regular potting on and pruning increases their life span and encourages flowers, foliage, and fruit. Training is essential for climbing plants, providing support and making an eye-catching feature.

## POTTING ON AND REPOTTING

Most plants need potting on (moving to a larger pot) every 2–3 years. Pot on if a plant is too tall for the size of its pot, if roots appear through the drainage holes, if growth is stunted and yellow (even when the plant is fed often), if frequent watering is needed, or if the rootball is congested. Plants such as *Clivia*, and all orchids, should only be potted on if they are "climbing" out of the pot.

Check all plants annually, potting them on in late spring before they begin to grow. New purchases may need immediate potting on. Make sure you are using suitable compost for each plant (see box left).

To remove most plants, soak the rootball by watering heavily, allow the excess to drain, then pull the plant out of its pot. You may need to slide an old kitchen knife between the pot and the compost or even break the pot to do this. An assistant might be useful to hold a large plant while you slide its pot off. If the roots are a solid mass, tease them outwards to encourage them to grow into the new compost. Use a sleeve of paper to remove a prickly plant from its pot.

### COMPOST TYPES

**HOUSEPLANT** *Peat-based compost; loam-based is good for larger plants.*

**COIR BULB FIBRE** *Peat-free mixture that provides good drainage.*

**CACTUS** *Contains slow-release nutrients; use for succulent plants.*

### CHOOSING A POT

Terracotta pots are porous, so plants in them are unlikely to be overwatered, while plastic pots retain more water, so plants do not need watering as often. Unglazed pots are not waterproof. Heavy clay pots are more stable for tall plants. Stand pots in a saucer to catch drips and avoid damage to furniture. For pots that do not have a hole in the base, use a deeper layer of drainage material, water carefully, and take care that they do not become waterlogged.

THE RIGHT POT

When it is time to pot on, pick a clean pot one or two sizes larger than the old one. Soak new terracotta pots overnight before use. Line the base with broken clay pot fragments, pebbles, or polystyrene pieces to help drainage. Place the plant in the centre of the new pot so the rootball is about 5cm (2in) below the rim. Fill between the pot and the rootball with compost, firming it in as you build up layers. When the compost is just above the rootball, water with tepid water and allow to drain. Stand the plant in moderate light for two weeks before moving into its permanent position. Do not water again until the compost surface begins to dry out. Repot plants in their old pots (see above) to restrict their growth.

REPOTTING
*Loosen the compost, replace the top 5cm (2in), fertilize, then replace plant in its pot.*

### HOW TO POT ON

TIME TO POT ON
*Protruding roots indicate this plant needs a new pot.*

REMOVE FROM THE POT
*Scrape off the top layer of compost from the rootball.*

PREPARE THE NEW POT
*Add drainage material. Cover with moist compost.*

FIRM IN
*Place plant in new pot and firm in with compost.*

## PRUNING

Keep plants under control with light pruning. This is ideally done in spring. Always cut back to an outward-facing bud or pair of buds. Cutting back hard to within a few buds of the base will encourage bushy growth and can regenerate plants that have become old and straggly. Trailing plants like *Tradescantia* or *Plectranthus* respond well to this treatment.

GETTING INTO SHAPE
*Pruning improves a plant's shape, thins tangled growth, and controls plant size.*

After hard pruning, reduce watering until new growth appears, and then increase as the stems lengthen again. Feeding plants with a general houseplant fertilizer will also help recovery. However, do not prune vigorous plants hard, unless you want to encourage masses of regrowth.

Soft, young growth can be nipped off with a finger and thumb or florists' scissors. This process, known as "pinching out", encourages a bushy growth habit. The material removed is a useful source of cuttings. Harder, mature wood should be cut off with sharp secateurs.

PRUNING TOOLS

SCISSORS    SECATEURS

Remove fading flowerheads immediately, or detach from the flower cluster. There are exceptions, like plants with ornamental fruit, or *Hoya*, which should not be deadheaded because the spurs on which the flowers form bear buds for the next flower cluster.

Finally, encourage well-shaped, healthy specimens by removing any signs of weak, diseased, dying, and dead growth, and any stems spoiling the shape by growing into the centre of the plant, as soon as they appear.

PINCHING OUT
*Nip off soft growing tips to promote bushiness and prevent straggly growth.*

### WHEN YOU ARE ON HOLIDAY

Stand plants on capillary matting or a substitute such as an old towel, and trail one end in a tray of water (left). Alternatively, make a wick from a cotton shoelace or string; dip one end in water and bury the other in the compost. Or simply group plants away from extreme heat or light and ask a friend to water them.

## TRAINING

The right method of training a climber will vary according to the plant's growth habit. Natural or coloured canes, used singly or in tripods, are popular supports. Secure the plant's flexible growths to the support with clips, or soft string or raffia (trim the ends neatly). Avoid fixing tightly around the stems. Thin stems of plants like jasmine can be twisted around wire hoops. At the end of the hoop turn the stem back on itself or carry on around. Prune annually and tie in new growth (see right). Plants can also be trained up trellis that is firmed into the compost or attached to a wall. *Cissus* and other plants with tendrils or twining stems will eventually cover the frame and support themselves.

REGULAR TRAINING
*Unwind straggling stems, prune, and resecure. Cut out old stems at the base. New growth will develop rapidly.*

Moss poles are good supports for climbing or twining plants, especially those with aerial roots and humidity-lovers. Make your own using a tube of chicken wire with crossed bamboo canes at the base. Fill the tube with moss and insert into the pot, surrounding it with compost. Always keep the moss moist. Pin aerial roots to the pole using hairpins or bent wire. As an alternative, wrap a thick layer of sphagnum moss around some narrow plastic piping, and tie it with nylon fishing line. Leave the base of the pipe free of moss so it can be inserted into the compost.

To display air plants, attach them to a piece of dead wood, pack sphagnum moss at the roots, and tie the moss in firmly with nylon line.

GROWING UP A MOSS POLE
*Permanently moist moss poles are the best climbing supports.*

### SUPPORTS FOR TRAINED PLANTS

BAMBOO TRIPOD
*Twine tendrils around the canes, tying in the stems.*

SINGLE CANE STAKE
*Insert cane with care to avoid damaging roots.*

SIMPLE WIRE HOOPS
*Two hoops are used here; add more if the plant outgrows them.*

# Propagation

PROPAGATING HOUSEPLANTS is a simple, cheap, and enjoyable way to add to your collection. Spring is the usual time for this, but many plants can be propagated at any time of year. The most popular methods are briefly outlined here; for individual plants, use the method suggested in each entry.

### TIP AND SEMI-RIPE CUTTINGS

Tip cuttings are taken from soft shoot tips, while semi-ripe cuttings have a firm base, yielding under pressure. Take cuttings from spring to late summer from non-flowering shoots. Cut with a sharp knife below a leaf joint, 7.5–10cm (3–4in) from the tip of a healthy shoot. Remove bottom leaves, and dip the stem into hormone rooting powder. Make a hole in a pot of cutting compost and insert the stem, lightly firming the compost around it. You can plant several cuttings in one pot. Water well and allow to drain, then label with the date and name and put the pot into a propagator, or use a loosely tied clear poly-thene bag. Do not cover cacti, succulents, or pelargoniums as they will rot. Place in bright light, away from direct sun, at around 18°C (64°F).

CHOOSE A SHOOT
*Select a healthy shoot that has not yet flowered. Cut straight across with a sharp knife.*

INSERT THE CUTTING
*Make a hole using a dibber, a pencil, or your finger, and insert. Firm the compost.*

Once there are signs of growth, remove the cuttings from the propagator and allow them to acclimatize for two weeks before moving to the plant's final position.

---

#### ROOTING A CUTTING IN WATER

Many plants will root easily in water. Prepare as tip cuttings, removing leaves below water level, and prop the cutting inside the container. Place in bright light, away from sun. If you use a glass jar, change the water regularly. When a good root system has formed, plant up and treat as tip cuttings. Handle fragile roots with care.

---

### STEM CUTTINGS

These are taken from the firm part of the stem, well below the soft growth tip. Using a sharp knife, make one cut just above a leaf joint, and another just under the leaf joint below it. Remove the basal leaves, then follow the procedure for tip cuttings.

### LEAF CUTTINGS

This method is often used to increase *Saintpaulia* and *Streptocarpus*. Cut a mature leaf from the centre of the plant, using a sharp knife. Leave 2.5–4cm (1–1½in) of stalk. Insert into the compost at an angle, until the leaf blade just sits on the surface. Treat as tip cuttings.

### STEM SECTIONS

Cut mature stem sections, at least 5cm (2in) long, with at least two leaf joints or leaf scars; even if buds are not visible, they will be stimulated into growth. Remove the leaves and press the sections horizontally into the compost until only the top half is exposed. Alternatively, insert them vertically into the compost, burying the end that was nearest to the base of the plant. Then treat as tip cuttings.

### DIVISION

This involves teasing the existing plant into sections, each with a growth point, leaves, and a vigorous root system; the divisions are then potted up (see right and below). Many plants form obvious divisions. If not, take the youngest sections from the outer part of the plant. A saw or sharp knife may be needed to divide old, woody plants. Divide in spring or early summer.

UNPOT THE PLANT
*Water the plant well, leave it for an hour, then ease it from the pot onto newspaper. Support the crown with your fingers.*

DIVIDE THE ROOTBALL
*Tease loose compost from the roots and divide the plant carefully at natural breaks.*

PLANT UP DIVISIONS
*Place divisions in pots and water. Give medium light and a little water until established.*

---

#### STORAGE ORGANS

Storage organs like rhizomes (right) and tubers can be divided. New growths like bulbils, bulb-lets, cormlets, scales, and tubercles can be detached from the main storage organ.

## LAYERING AND AIR LAYERING

Layering (see below) is used for many plants, such as climbers and trailers, that have long, flexible stems that root at the leaf joints. Detach from the parent plant when new roots have formed. Air layering is for more experienced propagators. Make an incision in the plant's stem and tightly enclose it in a polythene sleeve packed with moist sphagnum moss. Keep the moss moist and after about eight weeks, when roots show through the moss, sever the stem below the sleeve, discard the polythene, and pot up the plant.

LAYERING A PHILODENDRON
*Peg a mature healthy shoot into a pot of moist compost using a hairpin. Detach from the parent plant when roots have formed.*

## OFFSETS AND ROSETTES

Offsets are small plants that form around the base of the parent plant; many bromeliads and cacti produce them. Detach the offsets with a sharp knife, retaining as much root as possible, and dust the cuts with fungicide. Transplant them, and protect from direct sunlight until they are established. Some plants produce leaf rosettes that can be detached from the parent in the same way and grown on.

REMOVING AN OFFSET
*Look for a well-established offset, clear away the soil around it, and cut it off using a sharp knife.*

## PLANTLETS

Plantlets are small plants, produced on leaves or fronds, that often root in the compost around the parent plant. Detach or lift them with care and pot into moist compost. Some plantlets, borne on runners, can be put into a separate pot while still attached to the parent plant (right).

PROPAGATING BY RUNNERS
*Detach the new plant only when it is well rooted in its new pot.*

## SEED

Sow seed in spring or summer. Use a 9–12cm (3½–5in) pot, filled with firmed seed compost. Water well, or stand the pot in a tray of tepid water to two-thirds its height for about an hour. Allow to drain. Scatter small seeds over the surface and cover thinly with compost or vermiculite, or press larger seeds in gently so they are covered to their own depth in compost, then treat as tip cuttings. If you germinate seeds in an airing cupboard, remove them as soon as growth appears.

## HOW TO GROW FROM SEED

SOW THE SEEDS
*Scatter a thin layer of seeds and cover finely with compost. Firm larger seeds in gently.*

LEAVE TO GERMINATE
*Cover pot with a plastic bag or clingfilm. Remove when most of the seeds have germinated.*

REMOVE SEEDLINGS
*Place seedlings in bright light. Turn regularly. Remove when second set of leaves appears.*

PLANT THE SEEDLINGS
*Plant in small pots, holding them by the leaves so the stem and roots are not damaged.*

## SUCCULENT LEAVES

Succulents can be propagated from single leaves. Detach several healthy leaves from a plant, dust the cuts with fungicide, and leave in a bright position for two to three days for protective tissue to form. Insert the cut end of the leaf into a pot filled with one-third cutting compost and two-thirds fine grit. Stand in moderate light, keep the compost slightly moist, and transplant the new plants as they form.

## FERN SPORES

Remove a mature frond with brown, dust-like spores on the underside. Place it on a sheet of paper to shed its spores. Scatter the spores over watered peat substitute in a clean pot, cover with plastic, and stand in a saucer of water. Leave in a warm position and refill the saucer as necessary. After several months, small fronds will appear, each of which can be potted up.

# Houseplant Problems

HEALTHY HOUSEPLANTS that are well fed, carefully watered, and growing in suitable conditions are less likely to have problems with pests and diseases than those that are weakened through neglect or stress. Check new plants daily for the first few weeks for signs of pests or diseases, isolating them if problems arise. Once established, examine them regularly and deal with problems promptly.

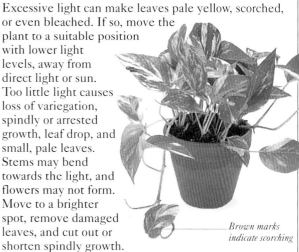

*Discoloured yellow leaves*

### OVERWATERING

Overwatering may be the cause if your plant wilts, the stems and leaves rot, growth is poor, or moss grows on the compost surface. It is certainly a problem for most plants left standing in water. To correct waterlogging, stop watering and take the plant out of the pot. Replace it when the excess moisture has dried out, then water as necessary.

*Moss on compost surface*

*Excess water left in saucer*

*Rotten leaves*

### UNDERWATERING

If your plant wilts, has falling leaves, and flowers that fade and drop rapidly, under-watering is probably the cause. It is definitely the case if the compost shrinks from the sides of the pot. To revive a parched plant, soak it thoroughly, breaking up the compost first to allow water to penetrate (see p.15). Then follow the correct watering regime.

*Limp, wilted stems and leaves*

### OVER- AND UNDERFEEDING

Overfeeding can be the cause of excessive soft, weak growth that is vulnerable to sap-sucking pests such as aphids and whitefly. It can also cause root damage, stunted growth, and scorched leaves. To correct these problems, return the plant to a suitable feeding regime. On the other hand, it is possible to starve your plants. Underfeeding makes growth slow or stunted, and leaves pale and lacklustre. Fertilizer may not be absorbed efficiently if plants are potbound. To avoid this, feed plants regularly when they are in active growth, and repot them as soon as they become congested with roots.

*Scorched leaves caused by overfeeding*

### YELLOW LEAVES

Yellow leaves may signal overfeeding, waterlogging, or draughts. If yellow appears between leaf veins, it shows a lack of iron or magnesium; feed the plant (give an acid-loving plant sequestrine). If an acid-loving plant's leaves are pale yellow, you may be watering with hard water or using a compost containing lime.

### LIGHT PROBLEMS

Excessive light can make leaves pale yellow, scorched, or even bleached. If so, move the plant to a suitable position with lower light levels, away from direct light or sun. Too little light causes loss of variegation, spindly or arrested growth, leaf drop, and small, pale leaves. Stems may bend towards the light, and flowers may not form. Move to a brighter spot, remove damaged leaves, and cut out or shorten spindly growth.

*Brown marks indicate scorching*

---

### ROUTINE MAINTENANCE

Inspect your plants as often as possible. Look out for any sign of pests or diseases, and deal with them as soon as possible if they occur. Remove the whole of any damaged leaves; if they remain they may attract fungal diseases. Once any flowers have finished, remove them and their stalks, or the stalks may rot in the centre of the plant.

PLANT MAINTENANCE
*Remove dead leaves as they spoil the general appearance of a plant and may also invite disease.*

## AIR AND VENTILATION

Browning leaf tips and shrivelling leaves and buds are usually caused by a too-dry atmosphere. Raise the humidity by misting or using a pebble tray (see p.15), or move the plant to a more humid location. However, dry, shrivelled leaves can also be caused by overwatering, underwatering, or draughts. In addition, brown leaf tips can be a sign of over-watering, underwatering, too-low temperatures, watering with cold water (always use tepid water), or potbound plants, so make sure you identify the correct cause before treatment.

Suitable ventilation is also important. Draughts can cause leaves to become yellow, shrivel, or drop, and

*Shrivelled leaves*

*Brown leaf tips caused by dry air*

leaf tips to become brown. If any of these becomes a problem, move the plant to a more suitable position, avoiding draughts and fluctuating temperatures.

## FLOWERING PROBLEMS

If flowers die very quickly, it could be due to over-dry air or temperatures that are too high. Correct these as necessary. If flowers do not appear, it is usually due to insufficient light, or feeding with too much nitrogen. If lack of light is to blame, give high potash fertilizer as well as more light. Moving a plant in bud, or keeping it at an unsuitably low temperature, can cause buds to drop. Prevent this by finding the plant a permanent home at the correct temperature.

## ARRESTED GROWTH

If plant growth stops altogether, light levels may be too low, or the plant may be starving or potbound. Nurse your plant by moving it to a brighter position, feeding it regularly with a high nitrogen or general houseplant fertilizer, and repotting if necessary.

## COMMON HOUSEPLANT PESTS AND DISEASES

The table below offers advice on identifying and dealing with the most common houseplant pests and diseases. Treatment with chemical sprays is often the most effective remedy for these problems. Some may need several treatments before they are under control,

so don't give up. When you use chemical sprays, always follow the manufacturer's instructions, and use an atomizer kept specially for chemicals. It is best to spray plants outside on a warm, still day, but remember not to leave them standing in hot sun.

| PLANT PEST OR DISEASE | APPEARANCE AND SYMPTOMS | CONTROLS | PLANT PEST OR DISEASE | APPEARANCE AND SYMPTOMS | CONTROLS |
|---|---|---|---|---|---|
|  WHITEFLY | Small white insects, found on leaf under-sides; brush the leaf and clouds fly up. They weaken plants by sucking sap and secrete honeydew, causing sooty mould. | Spray the plant with insecticidal soap or use chemicals such as pyrethrum, permethrin, or pirimiphos-methyl. Vary the type of chemicals you use. |  MEALYBUGS | Grey-white or pink insects, to 4mm (⅛in), covered in white "meal", often found in awkward parts of the plant. They suck sap, secreting honeydew. | Spray the plant with malathion or insecticidal soap. |
|  APHIDS | Small sap-sucking insects, seen on soft growth and buds, that also shed white skins on leaves. They distort tissue, secrete honeydew, and transmit viruses. | Spray with pirimicarb or an environmentally friendly insecticide like derris, soft soap, or pyrethrum. |  DOWNY MILDEW | Infection causes yellow spots on leaf surfaces, with corresponding grey fuzzy mould below. Mainly a problem on soft-leaved houseplants. | Raise temperature and avoid cool, damp conditions. Remove any infected parts immediately, then spray the plant with a fungicide such as mancozeb. |
|  RED SPIDER MITES | Minute, pale orange mites. They cause mottling, becoming yellowish white, on leaf surfaces. Heavy infestations give the appearance of fine webbing on leaves. | Increase humidity – red spider mites flourish in hot, dry conditions. Spray with insecticidal soap or bifenthrin. | POWDERY MILDEW | Powdery mildew appears as grey powder covering the surface of buds, leaves, and flowers. Leaves become distorted, and eventually drop. | Improve ventilation, avoid dryness at the roots, and remove infected parts at once. Spray or dust with a fungicide: sulphur, mancozeb, or carbendazim. |
|  SCALE INSECTS | Flat, yellowish brown, shield-like scale insects are found on stems and leaves, particularly along main veins. They suck sap, secreting honeydew. | Remove insects with a soft, damp cloth. In spring, the mobile young can be seen through a magnifying glass; spray them with malathion or insecticidal soap. |  SOOTY MOULD | A black fungus that grows on the sticky, sugary secretions left by sap-sucking insects. Sooty mould causes weak growth and spoiled flowers and fruit. | Carefully wipe off the mould using a soft, damp cloth. Control sap-sucking insects like whitefly, scale insects, mealybugs, and aphids, as above. |

# FLORAL EFFECT

HOUSEPLANTS ARE bought for their flowers more than for any other reason, and the sometimes short-lived appearance of the blooms makes them all the more desirable. Always colourful, flowers invariably draw the eye, so choose them with care – a bowl of bulbs can enliven a plain windowsill, while a single bold flower can transform a dull room.

*Ixora* 'Jacqueline' for summer flowers

△ WINTER AND SPRING FLOWERS *Daffodils, hyacinths, and primroses, grouped in shallow bowls, provide bright colour and delicious spring fragrance.*

Flowering plants have many points of interest: flower shape, colour, and scent can all turn a houseplant into an eye-catching feature. Bold-coloured flowers bring a cheerful note to a formal room, while those in paler shades can enhance a brighter background or subtly lighten a darker colour scheme. Some flowers offer the bonus of a delicious scent. It is worth thinking carefully before you decide where to place these plants, making sure they are accessible enough for the fragrance to be fully savoured.

Among the most varied attributes of flowering plants are the shapes and sizes of their flowerheads. These range from large, flattened heads of daisy flowers, long, tubular bells, wide trumpets, and tiny stars, to tall spikes, showers, and variously branched clusters.

## SEASONAL PERFORMANCE

If you only have room for a few flowering plants, then choose those that bloom continuously or over a long season, or those whose flowers are long-lasting. Remember that you can encourage some plants to flower more than once by careful pruning or deadheading. However, don't forget those hardy house-plants and bulbs that can be planted outside in the garden after they have flowered, where they will give many years more pleasure.

Flowering houseplants are now available all year round, and are often forced to flower outside their natural season. Some are sold solely for one season's flowering display, after which they are thrown away; this may seem wasteful to many keen indoor gardeners. Some, like poinsettias and Cape heaths, can be kept alive to flower again – it is tricky to accomplish, but with patience and care it can be done.

△ BRIGHT COLOUR *This begonia and calceolaria group makes a strong focal point, complemented by the tiny foliage of a compact mind-your-own-business.*

◁ WINDOWSILL COLLECTION *Most flowering houseplants love light, and these popular African violets are no exception.*

▷ STRIKING SPECIMENS *Beautifully shaped and coloured flowers, interesting foliage, and an elegant form make these zantedeschias perfect feature plants.*

# Houseplants with Fragrant Flowers

MOST OF US APPRECIATE fragrance in flowers, and there are many fragrant-flowered house-plants. Ideally, they should be sited so that their perfume can be relished at close hand. To enjoy them to the full, place them alone as specimens, rather than mixing different kinds of fragrance in the same room, and remember that their perfume may be overpowering in a small, warm room.

△ *Boronia megastigma*
**BROWN BORONIA**
‡ 1m (3ft) or more ↔ 60cm (2ft) or more

An erect, densely twiggy Australian bush clothed in narrow, aromatic leaves and, in spring, nodding, bell-shaped, scented, reddish-brown flowers, yellow within.

☼ Bright, but avoid summer sun ‡ Moderate to warm. Moderate humidity ◐ Every three weeks, using fertilizer for ericaceous plants ◊ When dry. Water sparingly in winter ▨ Semi-ripe cuttings

*Freesia* 'Blue Heaven' ▷
**FLORISTS' FREESIA**
‡ 40cm (16in) ↔ 25cm (10in)

This South African perennial has flat, pointed leaves, and produces sprays of richly fragrant white flowers, tinted blue-mauve, from late winter to early spring.

☼ Bright, but avoid summer sun ‡ Warm, but cool in dormancy. Moderate humidity ◐ Fortnightly as buds form, using flowering houseplant fertilizer ◊ Sparingly, increase when in growth, then reduce ▨ Cormlets

△ *Exacum affine*
**ARABIAN VIOLET**
‡ ↔ 20cm (8in)

From the Yemen, this pleasing member of the gentian family is compact and bushy, with shiny leaves and blue, pink, or white, scented summer flowers. Treat as annual.

☼ Bright, but avoid summer sun ‡ Warm. Moderate to high humidity ◐ Fortnightly ◊ Water when compost surface just dry. Reduce watering in winter ▨ Seed

**OTHER HOUSEPLANTS WITH FRAGRANT FLOWERS**

*Boronia megastigma* 'Heaven Scent'
*Brugmansia* x *candida*
*Cytisus* x *spachianus*
*Eucharis amazonica*
*Freesia refracta*
*Heliotropium* 'Chatsworth'
*Hoya carnosa*
*Nerium oleander*
*Plumeria rubra*

◁ *Gardenia augusta* cultivars
**GARDENIA**
‡ ↔ 1m (3ft)

Few plants have a more exotic fragrance than these. Large, fully double, white to cream flowers show in summer and autumn, set on a bushy, evergreen shrub.

☼ Bright, but avoid summer sun ‡ Warm. Moderate to high humidity ◐ Half-strength fertilizer for flowering ericaceous plants, when watering. Rarely in winter ◊ When dry ▨ Semi-ripe cuttings

△ *Hyacinthus orientalis* hybrids
## HYACINTH
↕ 20cm (8in) ↔ 10cm (4in)

Hyacinths' unrivalled rich fragrance makes them superb for a late winter or spring display. Hybrids are available in various colours; plant out after flowering.

☼ Bright to moderate, with some sun ▯ Cool to moderate. Moderate humidity ◖ Every three weeks ◊ Sparingly, increase as growth appears, keep moist in full growth, and reduce as leaves die ▭ Offsets

△ *Lilium longiflorum*
## EASTER LILY
↕ 90cm (3ft) ↔ 50cm (20in)

Large, trumpet-shaped, white summer flowers are richly fragrant. Widely grown for cut flowers, but an ideal winter pot plant if removed to a garden room. ♈

☼ Bright to moderate. Avoid sun ▯ Moderate to warm. Moderate humidity ◖ Fortnightly as buds appear ◊ Sparingly, keep moist in growth, and reduce as leaves die ▭ Seed, scales, bulbils

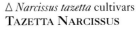

△ *Narcissus tazetta* cultivars
## TAZETTA NARCISSUS
↕ 50cm (20in) ↔ 15cm (6in)

Many scented cultivars flower from late autumn to spring. Force them for early flowering; afterwards, keep them in a garden room or plant out in a warm spot.

☼ Bright to moderate. Likes some sun ▯ Cool to moderate. Moderate humidity ◖ Fortnightly ◊ Sparingly, increase as growth appears, keep moist in full growth, and reduce as leaves die ▭ Offsets

---

### OTHER TEMPORARY HOUSEPLANTS WITH FRAGRANT FLOWERS

*Convallaria majalis*
*Iris reticulata*, see p.102
*Matthiola incana* (Brompton Stock)
*Narcissus* 'Soleil d'Or'
*Nemesia* 'Fragrant Cloud'
*Viola odorata*

---

*Jasminum polyanthum* ▷
## PINK JASMINE
↕ 2m (6ft) or more
↔ 1m (3ft) or more

This vigorous, twining shrub, with attractive, dark evergreen leaves, is easily trained to a frame. Richly fragrant, pink-budded white flowers appear from late winter to spring. ♈

☼ Bright to moderate. Likes some sun ▯ Moderate, avoiding fluctuating temperatures and cool draughts. Moderate humidity ◖ Fortnightly ◊ Keep moist, but avoid waterlogging. In winter, water when dry ▭ Semi-ripe cuttings

◁ *Stephanotis floribunda*
## BRIDAL WREATH
↕ 2m (6ft) or more
↔ 30cm (12in) or more

A strong-growing, evergreen, twining shrub best kept small by pruning and training. Waxy, very fragrant white flowers appear from spring to autumn. ♈

☼ Bright, but avoid summer sun ▯ Warm. Dislikes draughts and fluctuating temperatures. Moderate to high humidity ◖ Fortnightly. Occasionally in winter ◊ When compost surface dry ▭ Tip cuttings, seed

# Houseplants with Long-lasting Flowers

Plants whose flowers are long-lasting, or whose flowering is continuous or recurrent, are a bonus and well worth considering. They offer good value for money, and are particularly useful if you have room for only one flowering house-plant, or if you wish to add a reliable spot of colour to a drab, colourless location. Such plants perform best with regular deadheading, and in a position which offers cooler temperatures but which also benefits from good light.

◁ *Achimenes* hybrids
**HOT WATER PLANT**
↕ ↔ 30cm (12in)

Although the individual flowers are short-lived, with regular deadheading these attractive plants will bloom for weeks from summer into autumn. They are available in many colours.

☼ Bright, but avoid summer sun ‖ Warm. Moderate humidity ♦ Fortnightly, using flowering houseplant fertilizer ◊ Water freely in summer, reduce in autumn, keep dry during winter rest, and increase in spring ▨ Tubercles

△ *Anthurium andraeanum* 'Acropolis'
**FLAMINGO FLOWER**
↕ ↔ 60cm (2ft)

Breathtaking white spathes complement the polished, heart-shaped green leaves. The exotic flowers are produced through much of the year and seem to last forever.

☼ Bright, but avoid direct sun ‖ Warm, avoiding fluctuation. Moderate to high humidity ♦ Flowering houseplant fertilizer fortnightly ◊ Water when dry. Avoid waterlogging ▨ Division, offsets

---

**OTHER CONTINUOUS OR REPEAT-FLOWERING HOUSEPLANTS**

*Begonia semperflorens* cultivars
*Brunfelsia pauciflora* 'Macrantha'
*Catharanthus roseus*, see p.76
*Cyclamen persicum* hybrids, see p.32
*Euphorbia milii* var. *tulearensis*, see p.88
*Fuchsia* 'Swingtime'
*Hibiscus rosa-sinensis* cultivars
*Impatiens walleriana* hybrids, see p.87
*Spathiphyllum wallisii* 'Clevelandii', see p.83
*Streptocarpus* 'Kim', see p.63

---

△ *Begonia scharffii*
**SPECIES BEGONIA**
↕ 1.2m (4ft) ↔ 60cm (2ft)

Previously known as *Begonia haageana*, this hairy plant has bronze-green leaves, reddish beneath, and clusters of pinkish-white flowers through winter and spring.

☼ Bright to moderate ‖ Moderate to warm. Moderate humidity ♦ Fortnightly, using flowering houseplant fertilizer. Monthly in winter ◊ Water when dry, unless dormant ▨ Division, leaf cuttings

◁ *Aechmea fasciata*
**URN PLANT**
↕ ↔ 50cm (20in)

This splendid bromeliad from Brazil is well worth growing for its beautiful, strap-shaped, silvery-grey leaves alone. The long-lasting, dense head of sugar-pink bracts and mauve-blue flowers is produced in summer. ♈

☼ Bright, but avoid summer sun ‖ Warm. Low to moderate humidity ♦ Fortnightly, using flowering houseplant fertilizer ◊ When dry. Water sparingly in winter. Keep "urn" topped up in summer ▨ Offsets

*Pink-flushed cream flowers*

△ *Cymbidium* Showgirl
**CYMBIDIUM**
↕ 45cm (18in) ↔ 60cm (2ft)

Relatively easy to grow, this terrestrial orchid produces long-lasting flowers over a lengthy period in winter and spring. Showgirl is a deservedly popular variety because of its many flower spikes. ▽

☼ Bright. Needs some winter sun ▯ Moderate to warm. Moderate humidity ◐ Fortnightly, using half-strength flowering houseplant fertilizer. Monthly in winter ◊ Keep moist. Reduce in winter ▱ Division

△ *Kalanchoe blossfeldiana* 'Debbie'
**KALANCHOE**
↕ ↔ 40cm (16in)

A compact, shrub-like houseplant with large, succulent, red-margined green leaves. For many weeks, from winter through to summer, this kalanchoe is topped with dense heads of small, deep coral-pink flowers.

☼ Bright, with some direct sun ▯ Moderate to warm. Low humidity ◐ Feed every three weeks ◊ Water when compost surface dry ▱ Leaf cuttings

△ *Impatiens niamniamensis* 'Congo Cockatoo'
**BUSY LIZZIE**
↕ 60cm (2ft) ↔ 30cm (12in)

Curiously-shaped, red-and-yellow flowers appear at any time of the year on this succulent plant from tropical Africa. A short-lived houseplant with novelty value.

☼ Bright ▯ Warm. Moderate to high humidity ◐ Fortnightly. Occasionally in winter ◊ Water when compost surface dry ▱ Tip cuttings, seed. Roots easily in water

◁ x *Doritaenopsis* Andrew
**HYBRID MOTH ORCHID**
↕ 60cm (2ft) ↔ 30cm (12in)

A fine orchid, with a basal rosette of fleshy leaves that is topped, throughout most of the year, by a sparsely-branched spike of beautifully-formed, pale pink and rose-pink, long-lived flowers.

☼ Bright, but avoid scorching sun ▯ Moderate to warm, avoiding draughts. High humidity ◐ Fortnightly, using half-strength orchid fertilizer ◊ Keep moist, but avoid waterlogging ▱ Plantlets

**OTHER HOUSEPLANTS WITH LONG-LASTING FLOWERS**

*Anthurium scherzerianum* 'Sunshine', see p.34
*Aphelandra squarrosa* 'Dania', see p.70
*Celosia argentea* Olympia Series
*Cymbidium* hybrids, see p.112
*Cymbidium* mini hybrids
*Gerbera jamesonii* cultivars
*Phalaenopsis* hybrids, see p.113

△ *Saintpaulia* 'Bright Eyes'
**AFRICAN VIOLET**
↕ ↔ 15cm (6in)

African violets are among the most popular of all flowering houseplants. This neat, deep purple variety will produce flowers virtually all year round. ▽

☼ Bright to moderate. Avoid sun ▯ Moderate to warm. Avoid fluctuation. Moderate to high humidity ◐ Fortnightly, using African violet fertilizer. Monthly in winter ◊ When just dry ▱ Division, leaf cuttings

# Houseplants with Bold-coloured Flowers

BOLD-COLOURED FLOWERS always attract attention, so they need to be placed with extra care and thought. They should be eye-catching but not distracting, and welcoming but not overwhelming. The bright colours of the plants featured here can be used to transform a sparsely furnished or uninspiring room, or effectively displayed as bold specimen houseplants.

### *Begonia* 'Batik' ▷
### WINTER-FLOWERING BEGONIA
↕ 23cm (9in) ↔ 20cm (8in)

Crowded, rose-like, double apricot-pink flowers top the glossy leaves of this neat and compact begonia from late autumn to early spring. Show it off on a windowsill.

☼ Bright to moderate, avoiding summer sun ≋ Moderate to warm. Moderate humidity ◖ Fortnightly, using flowering houseplant fertilizer. Monthly in winter ◖ When dry. Stop watering if dormant in winter ⚱ Division, tip cuttings

△ *Clivia miniata*
### CLIVIA, KAFFIR LILY
↕ ↔ 50cm (20in)

This robust South African perennial is available in several colours; the flowers appear in spring, especially if the plant is pot-bound. Needs a winter rest. ♔

☼ Bright. Avoid summer sun ≋ Moderate to warm. Moderate humidity ◖ Fortnightly, using flowering houseplant fertilizer. Occasionally in winter ◖ When just dry. Water sparingly in winter ⚱ Division, seed

---

### OTHER HOUSEPLANTS WITH BOLD-COLOURED FLOWERS

*Begonia* 'Illumination Orange'
*Canna* 'Lucifer'
*Chrysanthemum* 'Golden Chalice'
*Cyrtanthus elatus*
*Gerbera* Sunburst Series
*Nopalxochia ackermannii*
*Pericallis* x *hybrida* 'Spring Glory'
*Sinningia* 'Waterloo'

---

*Intense magenta bracts*

### *Bougainvillea* 'Alexandra' ▷
### BOUGAINVILLEA, PAPER FLOWER
↕ ↔ 1m (3ft) or more

Few houseplants evoke the Mediterranean and the tropics better than this thorny scrambler, whose bracts last from summer to autumn. A situation in plenty of light will give best results.

☼ Bright, with some sun ≋ Moderate to warm. Low to moderate humidity ◖ Fortnightly, using flowering houseplant fertilizer ◖ When just dry. Water sparingly in winter ⚱ Tip cuttings

### *Calceolaria* Herbeohybrida Group ▷
### SLIPPER FLOWER
↕ 23cm (9in) ↔ 16cm (6in)

Spring is the time when these curious, blotched, pouched flowers appear, in a range of rich, bright colours. A Victorian favourite, it is best grown on a pebble tray.

☼ Bright, but avoid summer sun ≋ Moderate. Moderate to high humidity ◖ Fortnightly, using half-strength general houseplant fertilizer ◖ Keep moist. Do not let the compost dry out ⚱ Seed

*Euphorbia pulcherrima* 'Lilo' ▷
### MEXICAN FLAME TREE, POINSETTIA

↕ ↔ 50cm (20in)

These popular shrubs with
their flamboyant winter
bracts are often viewed
as temporary plants but,
with patience, they can be
encouraged to flower for a
second year or more.

☀ Bright ❊ Warm, avoiding
draughts and fluctuation. Moderate to
high humidity ♦ Monthly ◊ Water
when compost surface just dry. Avoid
waterlogging ✄ Tip cuttings

### OTHER SHRUBBY HOUSEPLANTS WITH BOLD-COLOURED FLOWERS

*Bougainvillea* 'Miss Manila'
*Bougainvillea* 'Scarlett O'Hara'
*Euphorbia pulcherrima* 'Menorca'
*Hibiscus rosa-sinensis* 'Scarlet Giant',
   see p.61
*Hydrangea macrophylla* 'Hobella'
*Nerium oleander* 'Mrs. George Roeding'

*Hippeastrum* hybrids ▷
### AMARYLLIS

↕ 50cm (20in) ↔ 30cm (12in)

A popular bulbous plant with stunning,
trumpet-shaped flowers. It is sold dry in autumn for
winter or spring flowering, and with care can be grown
for years. Needs summer rest after the leaves die. ♔

☀ Bright ❊ Moderate to warm. Moderate humidity ♦ Fortnightly
during leaf growth, using flowering houseplant fertilizer ◊ Water
sparingly as growth starts, keep moist in growth, reduce watering in
midsummer, and keep dry when dormant ✄ Bulbils

*Gerbera*
'Freya' ▷
### GERBERA, TRANSVAAL DAISY

↕ 65cm (26in) ↔ 35cm (14in)

Big, bold, long-lasting daisy flowers, borne
on strong stems, are the trademark of this
South African houseplant. It will flower
from late spring through to late summer.

☀ Bright, with some sun ❊ Moderate. Low
humidity ♦ Fortnightly, using flowering houseplant
fertilizer. Occasionally in winter ◊ Water when
compost surface dry. Avoid waterlogging
✄ Division, seed

△ *Kalanchoe blossfeldiana* 'Gold Strike'
### KALANCHOE

↕ ↔ 40cm (16in)

Golden-yellow flowerheads rise above a
mound of fleshy, toothed leaves from
winter into spring. Cultivars of this easily
grown succulent are sold in many colours.

☀ Bright, with some direct sun ❊ Moderate to
warm. Low humidity ♦ Feed every three weeks
◊ Water when compost surface dry ✄ Division,
leaf cuttings

*Hibiscus* 'Royal Yellow' ▷
### ROSE OF CHINA

↕ ↔ 1m (3ft) or more

Sun-loving and a popular choice
for windowsills, this plant will flower from
spring until autumn in the right place.
Numerous cultivars, in many colours and
with single or double flowers, are available.

☀ Bright ❊ Warm, avoiding fluctuation. Moderate to high
humidity ♦ Fortnightly. Stop feeding at lower temperatures
◊ When compost surface just dry. Water sparingly in winter.
Avoid waterlogging ✄ Semi-ripe cuttings

# Houseplants for Flowers and Foliage

PLANTS GROWN SPECIFICALLY for either their flowers or their foliage have a part to play in any decorative scheme in the home, but just as important are those that offer more than one attraction. Many houseplants are worth growing for both foliage and flowers; with beautiful leaves on show when the flowering season is over, they give you the best of both worlds.

## Anthurium andraeanum 'Carre' ▷
### FLAMINGO FLOWER
↕ ↔ 60cm (2ft)

Large, long-stalked, heart-shaped, glossy dark green leaves are joined at intervals throughout the year by exotic-looking flowers with shiny red spathes. A striking specimen plant.

☼ Bright, but avoid direct sun ≣ Warm, avoiding fluctuation. Moderate to high humidity ◖ Fortnightly, using flowering houseplant fertilizer ◊ Water when dry. Avoid waterlogging ▦ Division

## Cyclamen persicum 'Sylvia' △
### FLORISTS' CYCLAMEN
↕ ↔ 23cm (9in)

Just one of a range of cyclamen offering a stunning combination of beautiful flowers, freely borne in winter, and mounds of striking, silver- and green-zoned foliage.

☼ Bright ≣ Moderate. Moderate to high humidity ◖ Flowering houseplant fertilizer monthly in winter. Fortnightly in spring ◊ Keep moist in growth, stop when dormant, then water for regrowth ▦ Seed

## ◁ Calathea crocata
### CALATHEA
↕ ↔ 30cm (12in)

Handsome for its combination of striking, dusky dark green foliage with purple undersides and erect, long-stalked flowerheads with bright orange bracts. The flowerheads are borne in summer.

☼ Bright to moderate. Avoid direct sun ≣ Warm, avoiding fluctuation. High humidity ◖ Fortnightly, using foliage houseplant fertilizer. Monthly in winter ◊ Keep moist. Water when dry if cool ▦ Division

## △ Eucomis comosa
### PINEAPPLE LILY
↕ 60cm (2ft) ↔ 30cm (12in)

This is an attractive bulbous plant with a rosette of fleshy, pale green leaves and erect, cylindrical, dense racemes of late summer flowers. It is dormant in winter.

☼ Bright, with some sun ≣ Cool to moderate. Moderate humidity ◖ Fortnightly, using flowering houseplant fertilizer ◊ When dry, then reduce as leaves die. Keep dry in dormancy ▦ Offsets, seed

*Kalanchoe pumila* ▷
## KALANCHOE

↕ 20cm (8in) ↔ 45cm (18in)

This small, succulent subshrub produces white, bloomy foliage, perfectly matched in spring by pink flowers. An ideal plant for a windowsill or a hanging basket. 🏆

☼ Bright, with some sun 🌡 Moderate to warm, but cool in winter. Low humidity 💧 Every three weeks 💧 When compost surface dry. Water sparingly in winter 🌱 Tip or stem cuttings

△ *Senecio grandifolius*
## SENECIO

↕ ↔ 1m (3ft) or more

Big, bold leaves on purple-downy stems are crowned in winter by equally large, crowded heads of tiny yellow flowers. Allocate plenty of room for it to grow.

☼ Bright, with some direct sun 🌡 Moderate to warm. Low to moderate humidity 💧 Every three weeks 💧 When compost surface dry. Water sparingly in winter 🌱 Tip cuttings, seed

### OTHER HOUSEPLANTS FOR FLOWERS AND FOLIAGE

*Aechmea chantinii*, see p.68
*Aechmea fasciata*, see p.26
  *Begonia* x *credneri*
  *Episcia cupreata*, see p.100
  *Musa velutina*
  *Pelargonium* 'Mrs. Henry Cox'
*Strelitzia reginae*, see p.81
*Veltheimia capensis*

△ *Ledebouria socialis*
## LEDEBOURIA

↕ 13cm (5in) ↔ 8cm (3in)

Sociable is the word for this popular little bulbous plant with purple-backed leaves, which soon fills a pot with its offsets. The flowers are borne in spring and summer.

☼ Bright, but avoid direct sun 🌡 Cool to moderate. Moderate humidity 💧 Monthly 💧 When compost surface dry. Water sparingly during winter 🌱 Division, offsets

*Fully open flowerhead of* Medinilla magnifica

*Medinilla magnifica* ▷
## ROSE GRAPE

↕ ↔ 90cm (3ft)

A truly magnificent plant, producing big, glossy, boldly-veined leaves, and showstopping, pendent flowers in spring and summer. Warmth and humidity are vital.

☼ Bright, but avoid direct sun 🌡 Warm, avoiding draughts and fluctuation. High humidity 💧 Monthly 💧 Water when compost surface dry 🌱 Semi-ripe cuttings, air layering

*Zantedeschia elliottiana* △
## GOLDEN ARUM

↕ 60cm (2ft) ↔ 25cm (10in)

An elegant, tuberous perennial with lush, heart-shaped leaves topped in summer by slim, golden-yellow flowers. Hybrids are sold in pink, red, bronze, and orange. 🏆

☼ Bright, but avoid summer sun 🌡 Moderate to warm. Moderate to high humidity 💧 Fortnightly 💧 Keep compost moist. Reduce watering during the resting period 🌱 Division, offsets

# Houseplants with Winter or Spring Flowers

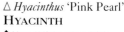

W INTER NEED NOT deprive you of the pleasure of flowers. Although it can be a dull season in the garden, many different houseplants will bloom at this time, including some of the most spectacular plants for the home, and some trusted favourites. Mass-produced plants forced on to flower need special care if they are to have a long life.

*Cyclamen persicum* hybrids ▷
### FLORISTS' CYCLAMEN
↕ 30cm (12in) ↔ 25cm (10in)

The gracefully swept back flowers of this hybrid rise above firm, beautifully-marbled, silver and green leaves. Hybrids come in many colours and enjoy cool conditions.

☼ Bright ⬛ Cool to moderate. Moderate to high humidity ◗ Fortnightly in spring, using flowering houseplant fertilizer. Monthly in winter ◗ Keep moist in growth. Keep dry in dormancy ⬛ Seed

△ *Hyacinthus* 'Pink Pearl'
### HYACINTH
↕ 30cm (12in) ↔ 8cm (3in)

Use several in a pot or bowl to display the dense heads of richly fragrant pink flowers. Other hybrids are available. After flowering, plant out in a warm spot. ♉

☼ Bright to moderate. Likes some sun ⬛ Cool to moderate. Moderate humidity ◗ Every three weeks ◗ Sparingly, increase as growth appears, keep moist in full growth, and reduce as leaves die ⬛ Offsets

△ *Erica gracilis*
### CAPE HEATH
↕ ↔ 30cm (12in) or more

A dwarf shrub from South Africa, with tiny, rich cerise flowers. Repot after it has flowered. It will not survive the winter if planted outside in cooler climates.

☼ Bright, but avoid direct sun ⬛ Cool. Moderate humidity ◗ Fortnightly, using ericaceous houseplant fertilizer ◗ Keep moist, but avoid waterlogging ⬛ Semi-ripe cuttings

*Euphorbia pulcherrima* 'Regina' △
### POINSETTIA
↕ 30cm (12in) ↔ 40cm (16in)

Strongly associated with winter, these Mexican plants are always popular. Red-bracted varieties are commonly seen; this compact white form is a welcome change.

☼ Bright ⬛ Warm, avoiding draughts and fluctuating temperatures. Moderate to high humidity ◗ Monthly ◗ When compost surface just dry. Avoid waterlogging ⬛ Tip cuttings

### OTHER FORCED BULBS WITH WINTER OR SPRING FLOWERS

*Crocus vernus* cultivars, see p.79
*Galanthus elwesii*
*Hippeastrum* 'Apple Blossom'
*Hyacinthus orientalis* 'Blue Jacket'
*Narcissus papyraceus*
*Tulipa* 'Oranje Nassau'

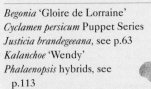

OTHER HOUSEPLANTS WITH
WINTER OR SPRING FLOWERS

*Begonia* 'Gloire de Lorraine'
*Cyclamen persicum* Puppet Series
*Justicia brandegeeana*, see p.63
*Kalanchoe* 'Wendy'
*Phalaenopsis* hybrids, see
    p.113
*Schlumbergera truncata*, see p.65
*Veltheimia capensis*

△ *Justicia rizzinii*
### JUSTICIA
↕ ↔ 45cm (18in)

Charming and reliable, this small shrub
has many small, nodding, red-and-yellow
tubular flowers in autumn and winter.
Also known as *Jacobinia pauciflora*. ♔

☼ Bright to moderate, avoiding direct sun
❄ Warm, avoiding draughts. Moderate to high
humidity ♦ Monthly ◊ Keep moist, but avoid
waterlogging ▭ Semi-ripe cuttings, seed

△ *Lachenalia aloides* 'Nelsonii'
### CAPE COWSLIP
↕ 28cm (11in) ↔ 5cm (2in)

This bulbous perennial from South Africa
makes a pretty late winter and early
spring display when several are planted
together. Flourishes in a cool room.

☼ Bright, with some sun ❄ Moderate.
Moderate humidity ♦ Fortnightly in
full leaf ◊ Keep dry in dormancy,
increase as foliage appears, and
after flowering, water when dry
▭ Seed, bulbils

△ *Primula obconica*
### POISON PRIMROSE
↕ 30cm (12in) ↔ 25cm (10in)

This primula is a winner for a winter or
spring display, but note that the roughly
hairy leaves can cause a rash on sensitive
skins. It is available in a range of colours.

☼ Bright ❄ Cool to moderate. Moderate to high
humidity ♦ Fortnightly. Monthly in winter ◊ Water
when compost surface just dry. Avoid waterlogging
▭ Seed

△ *Kalanchoe* 'Tessa'
### KALANCHOE
↕ 30cm (12in) ↔ 60cm (2ft)

Arching, then drooping stems, with succulent, red-margined
leaves, carry clusters of pendent, tubular flowers from late winter
into spring. One of the best of its kind for indoor cultivation. ♔

☼ Bright, with sun ❄ Moderate to warm, but cool in winter. Low humidity
♦ Every three weeks. Monthly in winter ◊ When compost surface dry. Water
sparingly in winter ▭ Tip or stem cuttings

*Rhododendron* 'Inga' △
### INDIAN AZALEA
↕ 40cm (16in) ↔ 50cm (20in)

Azalea cultivars, very popular for winter flowers, come in many
colours; this one has pale pink-bordered, darker pink flowers. It
likes cool conditions, but do not plant outside in cool climates.

☼ Bright to moderate, with some sun ❄ Cool to moderate. Moderate to high
humidity ♦ Fortnightly, using ericaceous houseplant fertilizer ◊ Keep moist, but
avoid waterlogging ▭ Semi-ripe cuttings

# Houseplants with Summer Flowers

SUMMER IS A TIME when the garden is bursting with colour, so it is easy to forget about using flowering plants indoors. Of course, colour can be provided by cut flowers, but these are often short-lived, and there is a wealth of houseplants that flower in summer which, chosen and placed with care, will provide a long-lasting feature in any room. Remember that houseplants should not be exposed to the intense heat of the midday summer sun, although bright indirect light will do no harm.

△ *Begonia* Non-Stop Series
**TUBEROUS BEGONIA**
↕ ↔ 30cm (12in)

Winter-dormant, tuberous-rooted plants grown for their compact bushy habit, bold leaves, and large double flowers in a range of colours. They are long flowering.

☼ Bright to moderate ⫶ Moderate to warm. Moderate humidity ◐ Fortnightly in summer, using flowering houseplant fertilizer ◊ Water when dry. Stop when dormant ☒ Division

*Achimenes* hybrids ▷
**HOT WATER PLANT**
↕ ↔ 30cm (12in)

These bushy, sometimes trailing perennials are dormant in winter but produce a mass of leafy stems, with flowers of many colours, from summer into autumn.

☼ Bright, but avoid summer sun ⫶ Warm. Moderate humidity ◐ Fortnightly, using flowering houseplant fertilizer ◊ Water freely in summer, reduce in autumn, keep dry in winter, and increase in spring ☒ Tubercles

---

**OTHER SUMMER-FLOWERING HOUSEPLANTS IN BOLD COLOURS**

*Abutilon* 'Nabob'
*Celosia argentea* 'Cristata'
*Cyrtanthus elatus*
*Fuchsia* 'Mary'
*Hibiscus rosa-sinensis* 'Scarlet Giant', see p.61
*Pelargonium* 'Caligula'
*Sinningia* 'Waterloo'

---

◁ *Anthurium scherzerianum* 'Sunshine'
**FLAMINGO FLOWER**
↕ 60cm (2ft) ↔ 45cm (18in)

One of the most impressive of all flowering evergreens, especially when the brilliant, waxy red spathes appear above the bold leaves in summer. Deserves special attention.

☼ Bright, but avoid direct sun ⫶ Warm, avoiding fluctuation. Moderate to high humidity ◐ Fortnightly, using flowering houseplant fertilizer ◊ Water when compost surface dry. Avoid waterlogging ☒ Division

△ *Campanula isophylla*
**FALLING STARS**
↕ 20cm (8in) ↔ 30cm (12in)

A superb plant for a hanging basket where the leafy, trailing stems of blue or white flowers can be seen. With deadheading, it will continue blooming in autumn.

☼ Bright, but avoid direct sun ⫶ Moderate. Moderate humidity ◐ Fortnightly ◊ When compost surface just dry. Reduce watering in winter ☒ Tip cuttings, seed

### *Ixora* 'Jacqueline' ▷
### IXORA, JUNGLE FLAME
↕ ↔ 1m (3ft) or more

When the orange-red flower clusters
appear, shining above the dark
green foliage, this plant is
especially beautiful. It is tricky
for beginners to grow, as it hates
cold air, draughts, and being
moved, so once placed, leave it be. Pinch
out the tips to encourage bushiness.

☼ Bright, avoiding direct summer sun ▮ Moderate.
Moderate to high humidity ♦ Fortnightly, using
ericaceous houseplant fertilizer ◊ When compost
surface dry. Reduce in winter ▨ Semi-ripe cuttings

### △ *Eustoma grandiflorum*
### PRAIRIE GENTIAN
↕ 50cm (20in) ↔ 30cm (12in)

Also known as *Lisianthus*, this gentian
relative is generally short-lived but gives a
rich display of large, erect, satiny, bell-
shaped flowers above grey-green foliage.

☼ Bright. Likes some sun ▮ Moderate. Moderate
humidity ♦ Fortnightly, using flowering houseplant
fertilizer ◊ Water when compost surface dry. Avoid
waterlogging ▨ Seed

### *Saintpaulia* 'Mina' ▷
### AFRICAN VIOLET
↕ 10cm (4in)
↔ 20cm (8in)

These shocking pink
flowers are well worth
cultivating. A popular
summer houseplant, it
will in fact flower almost continuously
throughout the year. Saintpaulias can be
bought with single or double flowers.

☼ Bright to moderate. No direct sun ▮ Moderate
to warm. Moderate to high humidity ♦ Fortnightly,
using flowering houseplant fertilizer. Monthly in
winter ◊ When just dry ▨ Division, leaf cuttings

> ### OTHER SUMMER-FLOWERING
> ### HOUSEPLANTS IN COOL COLOURS
>
> x *Doritaenopsis* Andrew, see p.27
> *Hedychium coronarium*
> *Pachypodium lamerei*, see p.111
> *Plumbago auriculata*
> *Streptocarpus* 'Chorus Line'
> *Streptocarpus* 'Falling Stars'

### △ *Gerbera* 'Kozak'
### GERBERA, TRANSVAAL DAISY
↕ 65cm (26in) ↔ 35cm (14in)

Large, long-lasting, yellow daisies are
carried above a rosette of bold foliage.
This tap-rooted plant hates disturbance,
so repot with care. Other colours available.

☼ Bright, with some sun ▮ Moderate. Moderate
humidity ♦ Fortnightly, using flowering houseplant
fertilizer. Occasionally in winter ◊ When compost
surface dry. Avoid waterlogging ▨ Division, seed

### *Streptocarpus* 'Paula' ▷
### CAPE PRIMROSE
↕ 15cm (6in) ↔ 20cm (8in)

Cape primroses are from the same family
as *Saintpaulia*, and are almost as popular.
'Paula' has purple flowers with distinct
dark purple veins and yellow throats. ♔

☼ Bright to moderate. Avoid direct sun ▮ Warm.
Moderate to high humidity ♦ Fortnightly, using
flowering houseplant fertilizer. Monthly in winter, if
not dormant ◊ When dry ▨ Division, leaf cuttings

# FOLIAGE EFFECT

ATTRACTIVE FOLIAGE has great long-term value. Plants grown for their decorative leaves will give satisfaction all year round – an excellent reason to cultivate as wide a range as possible. Different houseplants produce leaves in a fascinating variety of shapes, sizes, colours, textures, and even scents.

△ TEXTURE AND FORM *Contrasting growth habits and leaf shapes combine to make this foliage group a pleasing whole.*

*Begonia* 'Merry Christmas' for silver or grey foliage

Leaves range in size from the selaginella's tiny scale-like foliage to the great leathery blades of a Swiss cheese plant. They also vary enormously in shape, from elegant, frond-like or plumed leaves to giant-sized, deeply-lobed or divided foliage. Plants with strap- or sword-shaped leaves are very versatile as they can fit into narrow or awkward spaces, and their strong vertical or arching shapes provide excellent contrast to plants of mound-forming or spreading habit, or those with broad or rounded leaves. Rough-, hairy-, or smooth-textured and aromatic leaves offer further variety in the home.

Foliage plants are also effective for adding detail above eye-level. Site trailing plants in indoor hanging baskets or in containers on tall pedestals or high shelves.

## A SPLASH OF COLOUR

Almost every colour exists in the world of plant foliage. Yellow, silver, red, or purple leaves provide an attractive foil or background for green-leaved plants. Colourful variegated plants also make superb single specimens. As a rule of thumb, pale or brightly coloured foliage "lifts" dark areas while dark leaves appear best against a pale background. Remember that green, the colour of most foliage, comes in an astonishing range of tones. Dramatic effects can be achieved with the different textures, sizes, growth habits, and shades of colour found on green-leaved plants alone.

△ SIMPLE STYLE *The small leaves of this delicate-looking pilea are eye-catching and add detail to the trailing stems.*

◁ COLOURFUL VARIETY *A red croton and bright-bordered coleus are set off by varied shapes and tones of green foliage, displayed at different levels.*

▷ DRAMATIC EFFECT *The narrow foliage of this gold-variegated croton makes a bold statement, providing a good focal point for a sitting room or bedroom.*

# Houseplants with Small Foliage

S MALL-LEAVED HOUSEPLANTS lend themselves to restricted spaces, particularly where they can be examined in detail, and can be a foil to larger-leaved plants. Those with a trailing habit, in hanging baskets or on high surfaces, will fill narrow gaps, while slow-growing varieties are effective in bottle gardens and terraria. Group plants of contrasting leaf shapes together in a large bowl, trough, or container.

### Begonia Brazil (new species) ▷
### BEGONIA
↕ 20cm (8in)
↔ 30cm (12in)

Small, rounded, fuzzy-textured, dark green leaves, marked with paler green veins, and with dark red undersides, form the crowded hummock of this intriguing, and as yet unclassified, begonia from Brazil.

☼ Bright to moderate, avoiding summer sun ⧯ Moderate to warm. Moderate humidity ◍ Fortnightly in summer, monthly in winter ◊ When dry, unless dormant in winter ▥ Division, tip cuttings

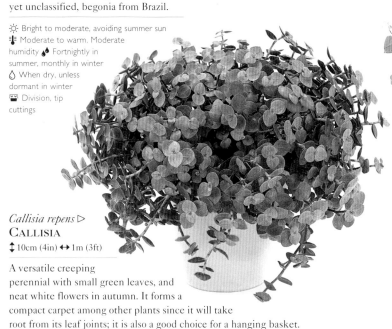

### Callisia repens ▷
### CALLISIA
↕ 10cm (4in) ↔ 1m (3ft)

A versatile creeping perennial with small green leaves, and neat white flowers in autumn. It forms a compact carpet among other plants since it will take root from its leaf joints; it is also a good choice for a hanging basket.

☼ Bright. Likes some sun ⧯ Moderate to warm. Moderate to high humidity ◍ Fortnightly. Occasionally in winter ◊ Water when compost surface dry ▥ Tip cuttings, layering. Roots easily in water

△ *Euonymus japonicus* 'Microphyllus Variegatus'
### JAPANESE SPINDLE
↕ 1m (3ft) ↔ 45cm (18in)

This hardy evergreen shrub, with bright, white-margined leaves, can be kept trim by pruning or pinching out. Slow-growing, it is suitable for use with creeping plants.

☼ Bright. Likes some sun ⧯ Cool to moderate. Moderate humidity ◍ Every three weeks. Occasionally in winter ◊ When compost surface dry. Water sparingly in winter ▥ Semi-ripe cuttings

△ *Ficus pumila*
### CREEPING FIG
↕ ↔ 80cm (32in) or more

The juvenile form of this evergreen is a useful houseplant, either clipped into a hummock or trained on a frame. Grown against a wall it reaches a good height. ♔

☼ Bright, but avoid summer sun ⧯ Moderate to warm. Moderate to high humidity ◍ Fortnightly. Occasionally in winter ◊ When compost surface dry. Reduce at lower temperatures ▥ Tip cuttings

△ *Peperomia rotundifolia*
## CREEPING BUTTONS
↕ 15cm (6in) ↔ 30cm (12in)

Best grown in a small hanging basket or in a pot on a high surface where the delicate trailing stems, studded with small, round, fleshy leaves, can be seen to advantage.

☼ Bright to moderate, with some sun ≣ Warm. Moderate to high humidity ◗ Every three weeks. Occasionally in winter ◗ Water when compost surface dry. Avoid waterlogging ▨ Tip cuttings

## OTHER TRAILING HOUSEPLANTS WITH SMALL FOLIAGE

*Aptenia cordifolia* 'Variegata'
*Ceropegia linearis* subsp. *woodii*, see p.92
*Dichondra micrantha*
*Ficus pumila* 'Minima'
*Hedera helix* 'Spetchley'
*Peperomia prostrata*
*Senecio rowleyanus*, see p.93

◁ *Streptocarpus saxorum*
## CAPE PRIMROSE
↕ 15cm (6in) ↔ 60cm (2ft)

Fascinatingly different from common Cape primroses, this east African species is prostrate in habit, and branched, with small, thick leaves. It bears charming flowers in spring and summer. ♔

☼ Bright to moderate, avoiding direct sun ≣ Warm. Moderate to high humidity ◗ Fortnightly, using flowering houseplant fertilizer. Monthly in winter, unless dormant ◗ When dry ▨ Tip cuttings

△ *Pilea depressa*
## PILEA
↕ 10cm (4in) ↔ 30cm (12in)

A creeping evergreen, with trailing stems bearing small, fleshy, bright green leaves. Display as *Peperomia rotundifolia* (above), in a small hanging basket or raised pot.

☼ Bright to moderate, with some sun ≣ Warm. Moderate to high humidity ◗ Every three weeks. Occasionally in winter ◗ Water when compost surface just dry. Avoid waterlogging ▨ Tip cuttings

## OTHER HOUSEPLANTS WITH SMALL FOLIAGE

*Aichryson* × *domesticum* 'Variegatum'
*Begonia* 'Queen Olympus'
*Cuphea hyssopifolia*, see p.80
*Peperomia campylotropa*
*Punica granatum* var. *nana*
*Saintpaulia* 'Midget Valentine'

*Saintpaulia*
'Pip Squeek' △
## AFRICAN VIOLET
↕ ↔ 10cm (4in)

This neat, compact African violet forms a tuffet of small, dusky green, dark-stalked leaves. Miniature, bell-shaped, pale pink flowers are borne throughout the year.

☼ Bright to moderate, avoiding direct sun ≣ Moderate to warm. Moderate to high humidity ◗ Fortnightly, using African violet fertilizer. Monthly in winter ◗ When just dry ▨ Division, leaf cuttings

△ *Tripogandra multiflora*
## TRIPOGANDRA
↕ 20cm (8in) ↔ 1m (3ft)

A loose hummock of trailing stems, with small, narrow leaves, is set off by white flowers, freely produced from autumn to spring. Best suited to a hanging basket.

☼ Bright, but avoid direct sun ≣ Moderate. Moderate to high humidity ◗ Fortnightly. Rarely in winter ◗ Keep moist. When compost surface dry in winter ▨ Tip cuttings. Roots easily in water

# Houseplants with Large Foliage

HOUSEPLANTS WITH LARGE FOLIAGE always make excellent specimen plants, particularly in larger rooms. Young, small plants can first be displayed as table centre-pieces, and moved as they grow. Large-leaved houseplants make superb focal points, especially when displayed against a plain background to accentuate their striking foliage and bold outlines. They can also be used effectively in a group of different plants, all with similar cultivation requirements but with contrasting shapes and sizes.

△ *Cordyline fruticosa* 'Red Edge'
**GOOD LUCK PLANT**
↕ 1m (3ft) ↔ 60cm (2ft)

This compact plant with broad green, red-margined leaves is best displayed in a group. Use the bold leaves to contrast with the surrounding furnishings.

☼ Bright, but avoid direct sun ▥ Moderate to warm, avoiding draughts. Moderate to high humidity ♦ Fortnightly. Monthly in winter ♦ Let compost dry before watering, particularly in cool conditions ▤ Division, tip or stem cuttings

△ *Anthurium crystallinum*
**CRYSTAL ANTHURIUM**
↕ ↔ 60cm (2ft)

A stunning foliage plant, producing large, velvety, dark green, white-veined leaves that are pink-bronze when young. It needs growing conditions similar to those in its native Colombian rainforest home.

☼ Bright, but avoid direct summer sun. Tolerates some shade ▥ Warm, avoiding draughts. High humidity ♦ Fortnightly in summer. Monthly in winter ♦ Keep moist ▤ Division

**OTHER HOUSEPLANTS WITH LARGE FOLIAGE**

*Codiaeum variegatum* var. *pictum*, see p.70
*Epipremnum aureum*, see p.92
*Ficus lyrata*, see p.97
*Philodendron bipinnatifidum*, see p.66
*Platycerium bifurcatum*, see p.109
*Spathiphyllum* 'Euro Gigant', see p.73
*Yucca elephantipes*, see p.87

△ *Cordyline fruticosa* 'Lord Robertson'
**GOOD LUCK PLANT**
↕ 3m (10ft) ↔ 60cm (2ft)

Green and cream leaves gradually turn red-purple with rose margins. Perfect for a richly decorated room, this elegant plant lives up to its aristocratic cultivar name.

☼ Bright, but avoid summer sun ▥ Moderate to warm. Moderate to high humidity ♦ Fortnightly. Monthly in winter ♦ Water only when dry. Reduce in cool conditions ▤ Division, tip or stem cuttings

△ *Dieffenbachia* 'Compacta'
**DUMB CANE**
↕ 1m (3ft) ↔ 60cm (2ft)

Dumb canes have beautifully mottled leaves, here with elegant cream markings. They have poisonous sap, so wear gloves to handle, and wash hands afterwards.

☼ Bright, but avoid direct sun ▥ Moderate to warm. Moderate to high humidity ♦ Fortnightly. Monthly in winter ♦ Water when compost surface has dried out ▤ Tip cuttings, stem sections

### *Fatsia japonica* ▷
**JAPANESE ARALIA**

↕ ↔ 2m (6ft)

Ideal for a cooler room, this bold, glossy-leaved aralia can be kept within bounds by pruning, and can be planted outside in most areas if it outgrows its allotted position.

☼ Moderate 🌡 Cool to moderate. Moderate humidity 💧 Fortnightly, using foliage houseplant fertilizer. Once in winter 🌢 When dry. Reduce if cool ✂ Tip cuttings, air layering

### △ *Monstera deliciosa*
**SWISS CHEESE PLANT**

↕ 3m (10ft) or more ↔ 1.2m (4ft) or more

Tropical South American rainforests produce this giant, popular for its vigorous growth and large, beautifully sculpted leaves. An impressive climber, it is best grown up a moss pole or trellis.

☼ Bright to moderate 🌡 Moderate to warm. Moderate to high humidity 💧 Fortnightly. Twice during winter 🌢 Let compost surface dry before watering ✂ Stem cuttings, air layering

### △ *Ficus elastica*
**RUBBER PLANT**

↕ 3m (10ft) or more ↔ 1m (3ft) or more

The bold form of their leathery, paddle-shaped, glossy dark green leaves makes rubber plants highly desirable specimens. Will eventually outgrow an average room.

☼ Bright to moderate 🌡 Moderate to warm. Moderate to high humidity 💧 Foliage houseplant fertilizer fortnightly. Monthly in winter 🌢 When dry. Reduce watering if cool ✂ Tip cuttings, air layering

### △ *Grevillea robusta*
**SILK OAK**

↕ 3m (10ft) or more ↔ 1.5m (5ft) or more

Silk oaks' large leaves are composed of leaflets that create a delicate filigree. In their native Australia they become huge trees. Grow in lime-free compost.

☼ Bright to shady, avoiding direct sun 🌡 Cool to warm. Moderate humidity 💧 Fortnightly, spring to autumn, using foliage houseplant fertilizer 🌢 When dry, using soft water ✂ Semi-ripe cuttings, seed

### △ *Philodendron erubescens* 'Imperial Red'
**BLUSHING PHILODENDRON**

↕ 3m (10ft) or more ↔ 1m (3ft) or more

The young leaves of this philodendron are deep claret, maturing to dark green, deeply veined and glossy. Bushy when young, it will climb when established.

☼ Bright to moderate 🌡 Warm. Moderate to high humidity 💧 Fortnightly, using foliage houseplant fertilizer. Monthly in winter 🌢 Water when compost surface dry ✂ Tip cuttings

# Houseplants with Narrow or Sword-shaped Foliage

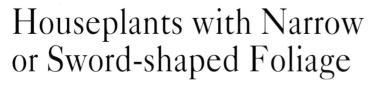

NARROW-LEAVED PLANTS can be very effective, especially when contrasted with broad-leaved subjects. Used with flair, many houseplants with sword-shaped foliage can contribute height to a group and break up hard horizontal lines in the display. As specimen plants, tall varieties can provide a strong focal point as well as being useful "fillers" in narrow spaces and awkward corners.

△ *Acorus gramineus* 'Ogon'
**JAPANESE SWEET FLAG**
↕ 25cm (10in) ↔ 45cm (18in)

Erect when young, this small, clump-forming perennial forms a broad mound of arching, aromatic, green- and gold-striped, narrow leaves. Colour fades in poor light.

☼ Bright to moderate, with some sun
🌡 Cool to moderate. Moderate humidity
💧 Every three weeks. Occasionally
in winter ◊ Keep
moist 🖤 Division

*Codiaeum* 'Goldfinger' ▷
**CROTON**
↕ ↔ 1m (3ft) or more

The long, narrow, gold-variegated leaves of this shrub, one of the colourful croton family, bring an exotic flavour to any room. It loves generous amounts of light, heat, and humidity.

☼ Bright, with some sun
🌡 Warm, avoiding draughts
and fluctuation. Moderate to
high humidity 💧 Fortnightly,
using foliage houseplant
fertilizer. Occasionally in winter
◊ Keep moist. In winter, water
when compost surface dry
🖤 Tip cuttings

*Leaves arch
with age*

*Carex conica* 'Snowline' ▷
**ORNAMENTAL SEDGE**
↕ 15cm (6in) ↔ 25cm (10in)

Quite hardy and suitable for an unheated room, this small, densely tufted evergreen is a useful houseplant with narrow, dark green leaves, margined creamy-white and arching outwards.

☼ Bright to shady, with some sun 🌡 Cool to
moderate. Moderate humidity 💧 Every three
weeks. Occasionally in winter ◊ When compost
surface dry. Reduce watering in winter 🖤 Division

*Cordyline australis* 'Red Star' △
**NEW ZEALAND CABBAGE TREE**
↕ 3m (10ft) ↔ 1m (3ft)

When young this plant produces a glorious, leafy rosette, but it soon forms a woody stem with leaves collecting towards the summit. An excellent window plant when young.

☼ Bright to moderate 🌡 Moderate to warm. Moderate to high humidity
💧 Fortnightly ◊ Water when compost surface just dry. Reduce watering in
winter 🖤 Stem sections

*Cordyline australis*
'Sundance' ▷
**NEW ZEALAND
CABBAGE TREE**
↕ 3m (10ft) ↔ 1m (3ft)

This striking plant from
New Zealand has long, narrow,
leathery leaves that form a wide
arch from the base. Young specimens are
ideal for a sunny window position.

☼ Bright to moderate ▮ Moderate to warm.
Moderate to high humidity ♦ Fortnightly ◊ Water
when compost surface just dry. Reduce watering in
winter ▦ Stem sections

△ *Isolepis cernua*
**SLENDER CLUB-RUSH**
↕ 15cm (6in) ↔ 45cm (18in)

A charming, tufted little
rush-like plant with
thread-like, arching or
drooping leaves and
equally slender
shoots bearing
tiny brown spikes.
Useful with small
bulbs or ferns.

☼ Bright to shady, with
some sun ▮ Cool to
moderate. Moderate
humidity ♦ Every three
weeks. Occasionally in winter
◊ When compost surface dry.
Reduce watering in winter ▦ Division

△ *Pandanus veitchii*
**SCREW PINE**
↕ ↔ 1.2m (4ft) or more

Like a pineapple in habit, except that the
white-margined, dark green leaves droop
at the tips. A dramatic houseplant, but it
has vicious spiny teeth, so place with care.

☼ Bright to moderate, avoiding summer sun
▮ Warm. High humidity ♦ Fortnightly.
Occasionally in winter ◊ Keep moist. Reduce
watering in winter ▦ Division, stem sections

*Magenta-edged
evergreen leaves*

*Dracaena cincta*
'Magenta' ▷
**DRACAENA**
↕ 3m (10ft) ↔ 1.2m (4ft)

Slow-growing and with
slender stems, this evergreen
will branch with age, displaying
its crowded rosettes of long,
narrow, arching leaves. Good
light gives the best colour.

☼ Bright to moderate,
avoiding summer sun
▮ Warm. Moderate to high
humidity ♦ Fortnightly.
Occasionally in winter ◊ When
compost surface dry. Water
sparingly in winter ▦ Tip
cuttings, stem sections

**OTHER HOUSEPLANTS WITH
NARROW FOLIAGE**

*Ananas bracteatus* 'Tricolor', see p.60
*Beaucarnea recurvata*, see p.96
*Billbergia* x *windii*, see p.116
*Cordyline australis* 'Albertii'
   *Dracaena fragrans* 'Janet Craig', see
      p.90
   *Ophiopogon jaburan* 'Vittatus'
   *Phormium* 'Cream Delight'
   *Phormium* 'Crimson Devil'
   *Tradescantia spathacea*
   *Yucca elephantipes*, see p.87

△ *Phormium* 'Sundowner'
**NEW ZEALAND FLAX**
↕ ↔ 1.5m (5ft)

Bold in habit and in leaf, this has tall,
erect, leathery, sword-shaped leaves, with
a dull purple centre and broad edges of
pink, fading to cream. A fine focal point.

☼ Bright to moderate, with some sun ▮ Cool to
moderate. Moderate humidity ♦ Fortnightly.
Occasionally in winter ◊ When compost surface
dry. Reduce watering in winter ▦ Division

# Houseplants with Textured Foliage

THE HUGE VARIETY of leaf surfaces that plants present to the touch provide a seemingly unending source of pleasure. Some leaves are rough, with distinctive ridges or wrinkles, while others have a smooth or velvety patina that begs to be stroked. Try using several of these in a feature group. People with sensitive skin should take care with bristly-leaved plants, which can cause skin irritation or a rash.

*Begonia* 'Beatrice Haddrell' ▷
**RHIZOMATOUS BEGONIA**
↕ 15cm (6in) ↔ 25cm (10in)

Worth growing just for its sharply angled, almost star-shaped, velvety, dark brownish leaves, which have light green veins and centres and deep red undersides. Sprays of pale pink or white flowers appear from winter into early spring.

☼ Bright to moderate, avoiding summer sun ☲ Moderate to warm. Moderate humidity ◖ Fortnightly. Monthly in winter ◊ When compost surface dry. Stop watering if winter dormant ⬛ Division

△ *Begonia masoniana*
**IRON CROSS BEGONIA**
↕ ↔ 50cm (20in)

An old favourite from New Guinea, the iron cross begonia takes its name from the distinctive dark mark in the centre of each bright green, puckered, hairy leaf. A stunning foliage plant. ♔

☼ Bright to moderate, avoiding summer sun ☲ Moderate to warm. Moderate humidity ◖ Fortnightly. Monthly in winter ◊ When dry. Stop watering if dormant in winter ⬛ Division, leaf cuttings

---

### OTHER HOUSEPLANTS WITH SMOOTH-TEXTURED FOLIAGE

*Anthurium andraeanum*
*Aspidistra elatior,* see p.88
*Asplenium nidus,* see p.108
*Begonia* 'Thurstonii'
*Codiaeum variegatum* var. *pictum,* see p.70
*Dracaena fragrans* 'Massangeana', see p.77
*Ficus elastica,* see p.41
*Veltheimia capensis*

---

△ *Begonia bowerae*
**EYELASH BEGONIA**
↕ 25cm (10in) ↔ 18cm (7in) ⬓

Easy to grow and very popular, eyelash begonias have crinkly-margined, dark-spotted, whiskery leaves. Grow them on a windowsill where they can be easily seen.

☼ Bright to moderate, avoiding summer sun ☲ Moderate to warm. Moderate humidity ◖ Fortnightly. Monthly in winter ◊ When compost surface dry. Water sparingly in winter ⬛ Division

◁ *Gynura aurantiaca*
'Purple Passion'
**PURPLE VELVET PLANT**
↕ 3m (10ft) ↔ 60cm (2ft)

Purple velvet is exactly what the leaves of this scrambling plant from Java look and feel like. To maintain a compact habit, train stems to a support and pinch out the tips. Nip off buds of the evil-smelling flowers when they appear. ♔

☼ Bright, but avoid summer sun ☲ Warm. Moderate to high humidity ◖ Fortnightly. Occasionally in winter ◊ Water when compost surface dry. Avoid overwatering ⬛ Tip cuttings

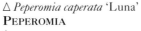

△ *Kalanchoe tomentosa*
## PANDA PLANT, PUSSY EARS
↕ 1m (3ft) ↔ 20cm (8in)

Everyone will enjoy stroking the soft, white, felted leaves of this Madagascan shrub; its shoots have the same texture. Avoid wetting leaves when watering. ♔

☼ Bright, with some sun ╣ Moderate to warm, but cool in winter. Low humidity ◑ Every three weeks. Monthly in winter ◌ When dry. Water sparingly in winter ▱ Tip or stem cuttings

△ *Peperomia caperata* 'Luna'
## PEPEROMIA
↕ ↔ 20cm (8in)

The corrugated surfaces of these neatly heart-shaped, deep red leaves are not easily forgotten. The foliage is set off by slender spikes of white summer flowers.

☼ Bright to moderate, with some sun ╣ Warm. Moderate to high humidity ◑ Every three weeks. Occasionally in winter ◌ When compost surface dry. Avoid waterlogging ▱ Tip or leaf cuttings

△ *Pilea* 'Silver Tree'
## PAN-AMERICAN FRIENDSHIP PLANT
↕ 20cm (8in) ↔ 30cm (12in)

Puckered, quilted, sharply toothed, pointed leaves, strikingly marked with silver on a bronze-green ground, form the low mound of this eye-catching plant.

☼ Bright to moderate, with some sun ╣ Warm. Moderate to high humidity ◑ Every three weeks. Occasionally in winter ◌ Water when compost surface just dry. Avoid waterlogging ▱ Tip cuttings

### OTHER HOUSEPLANTS WITH ROUGH-TEXTURED FOLIAGE

*Begonia gehrtii*
*Bertolonia marmorata*
*Fittonia verschaffeltii* var. *argyroneura*
*Geogenanthus undatus*
*Hemigraphis* 'Exotica'
*Nautilocalyx bullatus*
   *Pelargonium tomentosum*, see p.47
   *Peperomia caperata* 'Emerald Ripple'
 *Pilea involucrata*
*Pilea* 'Norfolk'
*Saxifraga stolonifera*, see p.93

△ *Pelargonium* 'Mabel Grey'
## SCENTED-LEAVED PELARGONIUM
↕ 35cm (14in) ↔ 20cm (8in)

Deeply cut and roughly textured, the leaves of this pelargonium are just waiting to be rubbed, which releases their rich lemon aroma. Small mauve flowers are borne in spring and summer. Easy to grow and propagate. ♔

☼ Bright. Likes sun ╣ Moderate to warm, but cool in winter. Low humidity ◑ Fortnightly, using high potash fertilizer ◌ When compost surface dry. Water sparingly in winter ▱ Tip cuttings

◁ *Sinningia* 'Mont Blanc'
## GLOXINIA
↕ 30cm (12in)
↔ 45cm (18in)

This warmth-loving plant bears large, fleshy green leaves with a smooth, velvety texture. The foliage is a perfect foil for the big, trumpet-shaped white flowers that are produced in summer. Gloxinias are available in many other colours.

☼ Bright to moderate, avoiding sun ╣ Warm, but moderate when dormant. High humidity ◑ Fortnightly, using flowering houseplant fertilizer ◌ Keep moist, but keep dry when dormant ▱ Division

FOLIAGE EFFECT

# Houseplants with Aromatic Foliage

FOLIAGE EFFECT

JUST AS FRAGRANT flowers are a bonus, so too are aromatic leaves; their scent gives a plant added interest and can freshen stale air. Place these plants where they can be easily touched, as some leaves release their aroma only when rubbed between the fingers. There is a wide range of pelargoniums with aromatic foliage, but the different scents they offer are best not mixed.

*Myrtus communis* ▷
**COMMON MYRTLE**
↕ ↔ 1m (3ft) or more

Famed since antiquity for its fragrant foliage, this plant also produces scented flowers from summer to autumn, followed by black berries. Traditionally, sprigs of myrtle are included in royal wedding bouquets. Keep small by pruning.

☼ Bright, with sun ▮▮ Moderate to warm. Low to moderate humidity ◐ Every three weeks ◊ When compost surface dry. Water sparingly in winter ⊡ Semi-ripe cuttings

△ *Pelargonium* 'Fragrans'
**SCENTED-LEAVED GERANIUM**
↕ 25cm (10in) ↔ 20cm (8in)

When rubbed, the sage-green, velvety foliage of this small, bushy plant releases a pine fragrance. Small white flowers are produced in clusters in spring and summer. A reliable plant for cultivating on a windowsill.

☼ Bright, with sun ▮▮ Moderate to warm, but cool in winter. Low humidity ◐ Fortnightly, using high potash fertilizer ◊ When compost surface dry. Water sparingly in winter ⊡ Tip cuttings

---

**OTHER HOUSEPLANTS WITH AROMATIC FOLIAGE**

*Acorus gramineus* 'Ogon', see p.42
*Boronia citriodora*
*Laurus nobilis*, see p.104
*Plectranthus amboinicus*
*Plectranthus madagascariensis*
*Prostanthera ovalifolia*
*Prostanthera* 'Poorinda Ballerina'

---

*Pelargonium crispum* 'Variegatum' ▷
**SCENTED-LEAVED GERANIUM**
↕ 45cm (18in) ↔ 15cm (6in)

A trusted favourite since 1774, with a stiffly upright habit and small, green and cream, crinkly-margined, lemon-scented leaves. Pale mauve flowers are borne in spring and summer. 🏆

☼ Bright, with some direct sun ▮▮ Moderate to warm, but cool in winter. Low humidity ◐ Fortnightly, using high potash fertilizer ◊ When compost surface dry. Water sparingly in winter ⊡ Tip cuttings

△ *Pelargonium* 'Graveolens'
**ROSE GERANIUM**
↕ 60cm (2ft) ↔ 40cm (16in)

Oil of geranium is extracted from the deeply-cut, lemon-scented foliage of this hybrid. It is bushy, but its strong scent makes it an ideal plant for a windowsill.

☼ Bright, with sun ▮▮ Moderate to warm, but cool in winter. Low humidity ◐ Fortnightly, using high potash fertilizer ◊ When compost surface dry. Water sparingly in winter ⊡ Tip cuttings

△ *Pelargonium* 'Lady Plymouth'
**SCENTED-LEAVED GERANIUM**
↕ 40cm (16in) ↔ 20cm (8in)

Known in cultivation for 200 years, this pelargonium has deeply cut, bright green leaves, margined with silver, which are eucalyptus-scented when rubbed.

☼ Bright, with sun ▐ Moderate to warm, but cool in winter. Low humidity ◗ Fortnightly, using high potash fertilizer ◗ When compost surface dry. Water sparingly in winter ▭ Tip cuttings

*Branched flower clusters*

*Attractive, heavily-veined leaves*

**OTHER PELARGONIUMS
WITH AROMATIC FOLIAGE**

*Pelargonium* 'Attar of Roses'
*Pelargonium* 'Copthorne'
*Pelargonium* 'Creamy Nutmeg'
*Pelargonium* 'Lilian Pottinger'
*Pelargonium* 'Little Gem'
*Pelargonium* 'Prince of Orange'
*Pelargonium* 'Village Hill Oak'
*Pelargonium* 'Welling'

◁ *Plectranthus oertendahlii*
**CANDLE PLANT**
↕ 20cm (8in) ↔ 1m (3ft)

A charming plant of trailing habit, with fleshy, rounded and scalloped, pale green aromatic leaves with white veins. White or pale blue flowers are produced intermittently throughout the year.

☼ Bright to moderate, with sun ▐ Warm, avoiding fluctuation. Low humidity ◗ Fortnightly. Monthly in winter ◗ When dry. Reduce watering in winter. Avoid waterlogging ▭ Tip cuttings

△ *Pelargonium* 'Old Spice'
**SCENTED-LEAVED GERANIUM**
↕ 30cm (12in) ↔ 15cm (6in)

Attractive pale green leaves impart a pleasant spicy aroma to this erect plant, which also bears clusters of white summer flowers. Fairly bushy when in growth.

☼ Bright, with sun ▐ Moderate to warm, but cool in winter. Low humidity ◗ Fortnightly, using high potash fertilizer ◗ When compost surface dry. Water sparingly in winter ▭ Tip cuttings

△ *Pelargonium tomentosum*
**PEPPERMINT-SCENTED GERANIUM**
↕ 90cm (3ft) ↔ 75cm (30in)

White or pale pink flowers, borne from spring to summer, complement the softly grey-woolly, peppermint-scented foliage. This robust plant may need pruning.

☼ Bright, with sun ▐ Moderate to warm, but cool in winter. Low humidity ◗ Fortnightly, using high potash fertilizer ◗ When compost surface dry. Water sparingly in winter ▭ Tip cuttings

△ *Prostanthera rotundifolia*
**MINT BUSH**
↕ ↔ 1m (3ft)

Brush against this bush and smell the minty aroma of its tiny leaves. Principally grown for its masses of small purple flowers in spring and early summer.

☼ Bright, with some sun ▐ Moderate to warm. Low humidity ◗ Fortnightly ◗ Water when compost surface dry. Water sparingly in winter ▭ Stem cuttings

# Houseplants with Red, Pink, or Purple Foliage

PURPLE OR SIMILARLY bright-coloured foliage houseplants can be used to provide a bold, dramatic effect, especially when set against a pale background or placed in combination with green, yellow, white, or variegated plants. Good light levels are usually needed to bring out the rich colours, so bear each plant's light requirements in mind when placing it.

△ *Hypoestes phyllostachya* 'Splash'
**POLKA DOT PLANT**
↕ ↔ 65cm (26in)

Named for the pale pink splashes on its thin and otherwise dark green leaves, this plant's colour is most vivid in good light, and may revert to green in poor light.

☼ Bright, but avoid summer sun ❄ Warm. Moderate to high humidity ❧ Fortnightly. Occasionally in winter ◊ When compost surface just dry ▦ Tip cuttings. Roots easily in water

*Begonia rex* hybrids ▷
**PAINTED-LEAF BEGONIA**
↕ 25cm (10in) ↔ 30cm (12in)

The cultivars and hybrids of this Himalayan begonia, grown principally for their ornamental foliage, exhibit a spectacular range of colours including several in purple and silver shades.

☼ Bright to moderate. Avoid hot sun ❄ Moderate to warm. Moderate humidity ❧ Fortnightly in summer. Monthly in winter ◊ When dry. Stop if dormant in winter ▦ Division, leaf cuttings

---

**OTHER BEGONIAS WITH RED, PINK, OR PURPLE FOLIAGE**

*Begonia* 'Enech'
*Begonia* 'Helen Lewis'
*Begonia* 'Merry Christmas', see p.54
*Begonia* 'Mini Merry'
*Begonia* 'Rajah'
*Begonia* 'Tiny Bright'

---

△ *Calathea sanderiana*
**CALATHEA**
↕ ↔ 60cm (2ft)

Found wild on Peruvian rainforest floors, this plant forms a bold clump of deep olive-green leaves, purple beneath and with rose-red parallel stripes, aging to silver, above. Short conical spikes of violet and white flowers appear among the leaves in summer.

☼ Bright to moderate, avoiding direct sun ❄ Warm, avoiding fluctuation. High humidity ❧ Fortnightly, using foliage houseplant fertilizer. Monthly in winter ◊ Keep moist. When dry in cool conditions ▦ Division

△ *Leea coccinea* 'Burgundy'
**WEST INDIAN HOLLY**
↕ 80cm (32in) ↔ 60cm (2ft)

This Burmese shrub, commonly grown in gardens in the West Indies, produces handsome sprays of deeply divided, deep red leaves. A very elegant houseplant.

☼ Bright, but avoid summer sun ❄ Warm, avoiding fluctuation. Moderate to high humidity ❧ Fortnightly. Occasionally in winter ◊ When dry. Avoid waterlogging ▦ Semi-ripe cuttings, air layering

*Flowers may be pinched out for compact habit*

△ *Oxalis purpurata*
**OXALIS**
↕ ↔ 15cm (6in)

The clover-like, purple-tinted leaves of this southern African plant are rich purple beneath. Cream, white, pink, or purple flowers appear in autumn and winter.

☼ Bright, with some direct sun ⊨ Moderate to warm. Moderate humidity ♦ Fortnightly ♦ When compost surface dry. Water sparingly in winter ▦ Division

△ *Solenostemon* 'Volcano'
**COLEUS, FLAME NETTLE**
↕ ↔ 60cm (2ft)

Coleus leaves come in many different colour combinations, including this green-edged deep red. Pinching out the growing tips will give the plant a compact habit.

☼ Bright ⊨ Moderate to warm. Moderate humidity ♦ Weekly. Occasionally in winter ♦ Keep moist, but avoid waterlogging. At lower temperatures, water as compost surface dries ▦ Tip cuttings. Roots easily in water

△ *Strobilanthes dyerianus*
**PERSIAN SHIELD**
↕ ↔ 60cm (2ft)

Beautifully veined bronze-green leaves, with silvery-purple markings above and purple undersides, distinguish this plant. Flourishes in high heat and humidity. ♛

☼ Bright, but avoid summer sun ⊨ Warm. High humidity ♦ Every three weeks ♦ Water when compost surface dry. Reduce watering in winter ▦ Tip or stem cuttings

△ *Peperomia obtusifolia* 'Columbiana'
**DESERT PRIVET**
↕ ↔ 25cm (10in)

The rich purple, fleshy leaves of this peperomia are a striking contrast to the popular, and more typical, green form. This is an excellent plant for a terrarium.

☼ Bright to moderate, with some sun ⊨ Warm. Moderate to high humidity ♦ Every three weeks. Occasionally in winter ♦ Water when compost surface dry. Avoid waterlogging ▦ Tip cuttings

**OTHER HOUSEPLANTS WITH RED, PINK, OR PURPLE FOLIAGE**

*Acalypha wilkesiana* 'Musaica'
*Codiaeum* 'Flamingo'
*Cordyline fruticosa* 'Atom'
*Cryptanthus* 'Pink Starlight'
x *Cryptbergia* 'Rubra'
*Gynura aurantiaca* 'Purple Passion', see p.44
*Hemigraphis alternata*
*Hypoestes phyllostachya* 'Vinrod', see p.100
*Iresene herbstii*
*Mikania dentata*
*Tradescantia pallida* 'Purpurea'

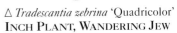

△ *Tradescantia zebrina* 'Quadricolor'
**INCH PLANT, WANDERING JEW**
↕ 25cm (10in) ↔ 60cm (2ft)

Vigorous, fleshy-stemmed, and easy to grow, this is ideal for a hanging basket or raised surface. The leaves are dark green, striped silver, and flushed pink and red.

☼ Bright, but avoid direct sun ⊨ Moderate. Moderate to high humidity ♦ Fortnightly. Rarely in winter ♦ Keep moist. In winter, water when dry ▦ Tip cuttings. Roots easily in water

# Houseplants with Gold- or Yellow-variegated Foliage

GOLD AND YELLOW are bright, cheerful colours for houseplants, and especially effective displayed against dark, plain backgrounds. Leaves with regular, marginal, or central markings are usually the most distinctive and dramatic, but spotted, blotched, or streaked variegation is also attractive; try combining several different leaf effects. Beware of placing these plants in low light conditions; with very few exceptions, this will cause the gold or yellow to fade.

## *Aucuba japonica* 'Variegata' ▷
### SPOTTED LAUREL
↕ 2m (6ft) ↔ 1.5m (5ft)

This tough, evergreen shrub with well-marked yellow variegation is an invaluable pot plant, suitable for cool or low light areas. Maintain a compact size by regular pruning.

☼ Bright to shady, avoiding direct sun ▮ Cool to moderate. Moderate to high humidity ◖ Monthly. Occasionally in winter ◊ When compost surface just dry. Sparingly in winter ▨ Semi-ripe cuttings

## *Dieffenbachia* 'Vesuvius' △
### DUMB CANE
↕ ↔ 90cm (3ft)

Boldly spotted, sword-shaped leaves make this tropical South American native a distinctive houseplant. Poisonous when chewed, so keep out of children's reach.

☼ Bright to moderate, avoiding summer sun ▮ Moderate. Moderate to high humidity ◖ Fortnightly, using foliage houseplant fertilizer. Monthly in winter ◊ Water when dry ▨ Tip or stem cuttings

---

### OTHER GOLD- OR YELLOW-VARIEGATED HOUSEPLANTS

*Abutilon pictum* 'Thompsonii'
*Calathea lubbersiana*
*Dracaena fragrans* 'Yellow Stripe'
*Hedera helix* 'Goldchild'
*Impatiens* 'Fanfare'
*Tolmiea menziesii* 'Taff's Gold', see p.79

---

## *Codiaeum* 'Gold Star' ▷
### CROTON
↕ ↔ 1m (3ft) or more

Colourful, glossy, leathery foliage makes this plant a striking focal point wherever it is used, but it is worth taking a detailed look too. Needs warmth and bright light.

☼ Bright ▮ Warm. Avoid draughts and fluctuation. Moderate to high humidity ◖ Fortnightly, using foliage houseplant fertilizer. Occasionally in winter ◊ Keep moist. When dry in winter ▨ Tip cuttings

## △ *Pelargonium* 'Mrs. Quilter'
### ZONAL PELARGONIUM
↕ 40cm (16in) ↔ 15cm (6in)

One of many bright foliage pelargoniums, reliable and easy to grow. Eye-catching, golden-yellow leaves have a distinct bronze zone that deepens in full sun.

☼ Bright, with some sun ▮ Moderate to warm, but cool in winter. Low humidity ◖ Fortnightly, using high potash fertilizer ◊ Water when compost surface dry. Sparingly in winter ▨ Tip cuttings

*Yellow-splashed leaflets*

*Peperomia obtusifolia* 'USA' ▷
**DESERT PRIVET**
↕ ↔ 25cm (10in)

This upright, brightly coloured evergreen plant, with large, fleshy, gold-variegated green leaves, is particularly suitable for a warm and humid spot such as a bathroom shelf. An attractive, versatile houseplant.

☼ Bright to moderate, with some sun ❄ Warm. Moderate to high humidity ● Every three weeks. Occasionally in winter ◊ Water when compost surface just dry. Avoid waterlogging ▭ Tip cuttings

△ *Sansevieria trifasciata* 'Golden Hahnii'
**SANSEVIERIA**
↕ 12cm (5in) ↔ 45cm (18in)

Quite unlike the familiar, erect *Sansevieria trifasciata* 'Laurentii' (see p.87), this bears dwarf rosettes of broad, fleshy green leaves with wide stripes of golden yellow. ♔

☼ Bright to moderate ❄ Moderate to warm. Low humidity ● Fortnightly ◊ When compost surface dry. Water sparingly in winter. Avoid waterlogging ▭ Division

△ *Schefflera arboricola* 'Yvonette'
**SCHEFFLERA**
↕ 1.8m (6ft) ↔ 90cm (3ft)

Use this tall schefflera as a specimen plant in a well-lit corner, or let it liven up a group of smaller, evergreen varieties. Prune it if a bushier habit is required.

☼ Bright to moderate ❄ Warm. Avoid fluctuation. Moderate to high humidity ● Fortnightly. Monthly in winter ◊ Water when compost surface dry ▭ Tip cuttings, air layering

△ *Pseudopanax lessonii* 'Gold Splash'
**PSEUDOPANAX**
↕ ↔ 2m (6ft) or more

Normally grown in its juvenile stage, when its long-stalked, five-fingered leaves are splashed with gold, this variegated pseudopanax makes a striking and individual houseplant. As the plant ages, the variegation on the foliage becomes less marked. Prune it to maintain a more compact habit. ♔

☼ Bright, but avoid direct sun ❄ Moderate to warm. Moderate humidity ● Monthly. Occasionally in winter ◊ When compost surface dry. Reduce watering in winter ▭ Semi-ripe cuttings

*Boat-shaped flower cluster*

◁ *Tradescantia spathacea* 'Variegata'
**BOAT LILY**
↕ ↔ 30cm (12in)

The handsome, yellow-striped leaf rosettes of this robust, clump-forming plant have contrasting rich purple leaf undersides. Unusual boat-shaped flower-clusters are produced throughout the year.

☼ Bright to moderate, avoiding direct sun ❄ Warm. High humidity ● Fortnightly. Occasionally in winter ◊ Keep moist. Reduce watering in winter ▭ Offsets

**FOLIAGE EFFECT**

# Houseplants with White- or Cream-variegated Foliage

VARIEGATED LEAVES add character to a plant; house-plants with foliage in cream and white, both neutral and versatile colours, can be used to great decorative effect. Variegation is usually found along leaf margins, but it is worth looking for bold stripes or unusual mottling. To emphasize the cream and white markings, display your plant against a plain dark background.

### *Acorus gramineus* 'Variegatus' ▷
### SWEET FLAG
↕ 30cm (12in) ↔ 45cm (18in)

The variegated leaves of this sweet flag, arching with age, have a delicate fragrance when crushed. An excellent plant for a cool room; likes damp compost.

☼ Bright to moderate ❚ Cool to moderate. Moderate humidity ◑ Every three weeks in summer ◌ Keep moist in summer. In winter, water when compost surface dry ▩ Division

### △ *Ficus elastica* 'Tineke'
### RUBBER PLANT
↕ 3m (10ft) ↔ 1m (3ft)

This rubber plant has many handsome features: dark grey-green variegation on the large leaves, cream leaf margins, and burgundy leaf stems and midribs.

☼ Bright to moderate ❚ Cool to warm. Moderate to high humidity ◑ Fortnightly, using foliage house-plant fertilizer. Monthly in winter ◌ Water when compost surface dry ▩ Tip cuttings, air layering

### △ *Aglaonema commutatum* 'Pseudobracteatum'
### CHINESE EVERGREEN
↕ ↔ 60cm (2ft)

Attractive variegation makes this elegant plant, from the Philippine rainforests, a useful specimen for a table display. It is slow-growing but well worth the wait.

☼ Bright to moderate ❚ Moderate to warm, avoiding fluctuation. Moderate humidity ◑ Weekly, using foliage houseplant fertilizer. Monthly in winter ◌ When dry ▩ Division, tip cuttings, stem sections

### △ *Dracaena fragrans* 'Warneckei'
### DRACAENA
↕ 2m (6ft) or more ↔ 60cm (2ft)

Lush and leafy when young, this plant slowly develops a strong stem. Popular with interior designers, it is an efficient remover of pollutants from the air. ♈

☼ Bright, but avoid summer sun ❚ Moderate to warm. Moderate to high humidity ◑ Fortnightly. Twice during winter ◌ Water when compost surface dry ▩ Tip cuttings, stem sections

### OTHER SMALL-LEAVED WHITE- OR CREAM-VARIEGATED HOUSEPLANTS

*Aichryson* × *domesticum* 'Variegatum'
*Ficus benjamina* 'Variegata'
*Ficus pumila* 'White Sonny', see p.65
*Glechoma hederacea* 'Variegata'
*Hedera helix* 'White Knight'
*Impatiens walleriana* 'Variegata'

△ *Hedera helix* 'Eva'
## COMMON IVY, ENGLISH IVY
↕ 1.4m (4½ft) ↔ 30cm (12in)

This attractive ivy, with purple shoots and white-margined leaves, will trail or climb; display it in a hanging basket, on a raised shelf, or even in a large terrarium. 🏆

☀ Bright to moderate 🌡 Cool to moderate. Moderate to high humidity 💧 Fortnightly. Once in mid- and once in late winter 💧 When dry. Water sparingly in winter ✂ Tip cuttings, layering

### OTHER LARGE-LEAVED WHITE- OR CREAM-VARIEGATED HOUSEPLANTS

*Ananas comosus* 'Variegatus', see p.116
x *Fatshedera lizei* 'Variegata'
*Fatsia japonica* 'Variegata', see p.72
*Monstera deliciosa* 'Variegata', see p.73
*Phormium* 'Cream Delight'

◁ *Syngonium* 'Arrow'
## GOOSEFOOT PLANT
↕ 2m (6ft) ↔ 60cm (2ft)

Compact and pointed green leaves, suffused with creamy variegation, change shape as they mature. Initially bushy, these plants become climbers with age.

☀ Bright to moderate, avoiding direct sun 🌡 Warm, avoiding fluctuation. Moderate to high humidity 💧 Fortnightly. Monthly in winter 💧 When dry. Reduce watering in winter ✂ Tip cuttings

△ *Hypoestes phyllostachya* 'Wit'
## POLKA DOT PLANT
↕ 30cm (12in) ↔ 23cm (9in)

A striking plant, grown for its marbled leaves. Good light will produce the best foliage. The flowers are insignificant, so pinch out the tips to encourage bushiness.

☀ Bright, but avoid summer sun 🌡 Moderate to warm. Moderate to high humidity 💧 Fortnightly. Monthly in winter 💧 When dry. Reduce watering in winter ✂ Tip or stem cuttings. Roots in water

△ *Plectranthus forsteri* 'Marginatus'
## CANDLE PLANT, SWEDISH IVY
↕ 30cm (12in) ↔ 90cm (3ft)

Display candle plants in a hanging basket or on an accessible shelf to enjoy their masses of fleshy, aromatic foliage. Pinch out the shoots to promote bushy growth.

☀ Bright, with some direct sun 🌡 Moderate to warm. Low to moderate humidity 💧 Fortnightly. Every six weeks in winter 💧 Let compost surface dry before watering ✂ Tip cuttings

△ *Tradescantia fluminensis* 'Variegata'
## INCH PLANT, WANDERING JEW
↕ 15cm (6in) ↔ 60cm (2ft)

Show off this delicate, pale green, white-striped foliage by trailing it over the edge of a container. Easy to grow; pinch out the growing tips to encourage branching.

☀ Bright, but avoid direct sun. Variegation fades in shade 🌡 Moderate to warm. Moderate to high humidity 💧 Fortnightly. Once in winter 💧 Keep moist. When dry in winter ✂ Tip or stem cuttings

# Houseplants with Silver or Grey Foliage

MANY OF THE MOST distinctive houseplants have silver or grey foliage. Some leaves take their colour from bands or stripes, while others gain their silvery appearance from a patina of pale hairs or a dense spotting or marbled effect. All the plants shown here will provide dramatic contrast when grouped with purple- or dark green-leaved varieties.

△ *Begonia* 'Silver'
**BEGONIA**
↕ 20cm (8in) ↔ 25cm (10in)

Curious but very attractive, this begonia has distinctive, long, pointed leaves, covered with tiny pale hairs that give the upper surfaces a silvery, satin-like sheen.

☼ Bright to moderate, avoiding summer sun ≣ Moderate to warm. Moderate humidity ◐ Fortnightly. Monthly in winter ◊ When dry. Stop if dormant in winter ▱ Division, tip cuttings

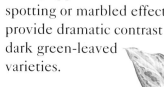

*Aglaonema* 'Silver Queen' ▷
**CHINESE EVERGREEN**
↕ ↔ 45cm (18in)

One of the most striking and dramatic aglaonemas, bearing large, pointed, long-stalked, almost wholly silver leaves patterned with pale and dark green markings. ▽

☼ Moderate, avoiding summer sun ≣ Moderate to warm. Moderate humidity ◐ Every week, using foliage houseplant fertilizer. Monthly in winter ◊ When dry ▱ Division, tip cuttings, stem sections

---

**OTHER HOUSEPLANTS WITH SILVER OR GREY FOLIAGE**

*Aechmea fasciata*, see p.26
*Aglaonema* 'Silver King'
*Astelia chathamica*
*Begonia* 'Salamander'
*Begonia* 'Silver Queen'
*Begonia venosa*, see p.56
*Cotyledon orbiculata*
*Echeveria secunda* var. *glauca* 'Gigantea', see p.86

---

◁ *Begonia* 'Merry Christmas'
**PAINTED-LEAF BEGONIA**
↕ 25cm (10in) ↔ 30cm (12in)

The large, jaggedly toothed leaves of this *Begonia rex* hybrid are strikingly marked with silver and dark red, and pink-flushed. Pale rose-pink flowers are a bonus in autumn and early winter. ▽

☼ Bright to moderate, avoiding summer sun ≣ Moderate to warm. Moderate humidity ◐ Fortnightly. Monthly in winter ◊ When dry. Stop if dormant in winter ▱ Division, leaf cuttings

△ *Ctenanthe amabilis*
**CTENANTHE**
↕ ↔ 40cm (16in)

This beautifully variegated foliage plant, from the rainforests of South America, has impressive green and silver zebra marks on its large, paddle-shaped leaves. ▽

☼ Bright to moderate, avoiding direct sun ≣ Warm, avoiding fluctuation. High humidity ◐ Fortnightly, using foliage houseplant fertilizer. Rarely in winter ◊ Water when top half of compost dry ▱ Division

OTHER HOUSEPLANTS WITH
FOLIAGE STRIPED, SPLASHED,
OR VEINED SILVER OR GREY

*Begonia maculata*
*Calathea makoyana*, see p.70
*Fittonia verschaffeltii* var.
    *argyroneura*
*Peperomia argyreia*
*Piper crocatum*
*Pteris cretica* 'Albolineata', see p.109
*Sonerila margaritacea*
*Strobilanthes dyerianus*, see p.49

*Ctenanthe*
'Greystar' ▷
**CTENANTHE**
↕ 1.2m (4ft) ↔ 1m (3ft)

A splendid houseplant with impressive foliage. The silver upper leaf surfaces are set off by contrasting dark green veins and stalks, while the leaf undersides are dark purple.

☼ Bright to moderate, avoiding direct sun ❄️ Warm, avoiding fluctuation. High humidity 💧 Fortnightly, using foliage houseplant fertilizer. Occasionally in winter 💧 Water when top half of compost dry ▦ Division

△ *Pteris ensiformis* 'Evergemiensis'
**SLENDER BRAKE**
↕ ↔ 30cm (12in)

This silver-striped cultivar makes a good contrast to other varieties of fern; it is even more attractive than the green form of this plant, a Victorian favourite.

☼ Bright to moderate, avoiding direct sun ❄️ Moderate to warm. Moderate to high humidity 💧 Fortnightly. Monthly in winter 💧 Keep moist, but avoid waterlogging ▦ Division, spores

△ *Peperomia caperata* 'Teresa'
**PEPEROMIA**
↕ ↔ 20cm (8in)

A charming plant that is perfect for using in a special display, bottle garden, or terrarium. The bronze-purple, puckered, rounded leaves are silvery-sheened above.

☼ Bright to moderate, with some sun ❄️ Warm. Moderate to high humidity 💧 Every three weeks. Occasionally in winter 💧 When compost surface dry. Avoid waterlogging ▦ Tip cuttings

△ *Pilea cadierei*
**ALUMINIUM PLANT**
↕ 30cm (12in) ↔ 21cm (8in)

Eye-catching, silver-splashed green leaves make this perennial from the Vietnamese rainforests a popular houseplant. Pinch out tips to maintain a compact habit. 🏆

☼ Bright to moderate, with some sun ❄️ Warm. Moderate to high humidity 💧 Every three weeks. Occasionally in winter 💧 Water when compost surface just dry. Avoid waterlogging ▦ Tip cuttings

△ *Soleirolia soleirolii* 'Variegata'
**MIND-YOUR-OWN-BUSINESS**
↕ 5cm (2in) ↔ 30cm (12in) or more

A useful small plant, with tiny silvered leaves densely crowding the branching stems and, in time, forming a creeping carpet. Good cover under large plants.

☼ Bright to shady, avoiding direct sun ❄️ Cool to moderate. Moderate to high humidity 💧 Every three weeks. Rarely in winter 💧 Keep moist, but avoid waterlogging. Sparingly in winter ▦ Division

**FOLIAGE EFFECT**

# Houseplants with Unusual Foliage

THE ATTRACTION OF the weird and wonderful is universal. Many of us who collect plants become fascinated by the search for curious varieties, particularly among foliage plants, which offer leaves in a range of different textures, colours, shapes, and sizes. Such plants make good talking points, so display them where they can be easily seen and studied.

*Begonia venosa* ▷
**SHRUB BEGONIA**
↕ 90cm (3ft) ↔ 60cm (2ft)

Large, kidney-shaped, fleshy leaves are covered with short white hairs, giving them a frosted appearance. The fragrant white flowers, produced from late summer onwards, are a bonus.

☼ Bright, but avoid summer sun ❄ Moderate to warm. Low to moderate humidity ♦ Fortnightly. Monthly in winter ◊ Water sparingly. Avoid waterlogging ✂ Division, tip cuttings

*Begonia listada* ▷
**SHRUB BEGONIA**
↕ ↔ 60cm (2ft)

A striking plant with large, dark green leaves, barred with pale green, pointed at both ends and shaped like out-stretched wings, one longer than the other. Bears white flowers in autumn and winter.

☼ Bright to moderate. Avoid summer sun ❄ Moderate to warm. Moderate humidity ♦ Fortnightly. Monthly in winter ◊ When compost surface dry. Reduce watering in winter ✂ Division, tip cuttings

△ *Begonia serratipetala*
**SHRUB BEGONIA**
↕ ↔ 45cm (18in)

Distinctive for its long-pointed, wavy-margined leaves, bronze-green marked with red veins above, and red beneath, this shrub begonia produces pinky-white flowers from winter to spring.

☼ Bright to moderate, avoiding summer sun ❄ Moderate to warm. Moderate humidity ♦ Fortnightly. Monthly in winter ◊ When compost surface dry. Reduce watering in winter ✂ Tip cuttings

△ *Codiaeum* 'Red Curl'
**CROTON, JOSEPH'S COAT**
↕ ↔ 1m (3ft)

Even if you have seen many variations of the croton, this one will amuse you with its long, narrow, corkscrew-like, colourful leaves. It looks well on its own or with green-leaved companions.

☼ Bright, with some sun ❄ Warm, avoiding draughts and fluctuation. Moderate to high humidity ♦ Fortnightly, using foliage houseplant fertilizer. Occasionally in winter ◊ Keep moist. In winter, water when compost surface dry ✂ Tip cuttings

△ *Cotyledon orbiculata* var. *oblonga*
**SILVER CROWN**
↕ 60cm (2ft) ↔ 50cm (20in)

This interesting shrubby succulent plant is dominated, especially when small, by its rounded, crinkly-edged, fleshy leaves, covered in a white, waxy bloom. Good for a sunny windowsill.

☼ Bright, with sun ❚ Warm, but cool to moderate in winter. Low humidity ◕ Monthly, using fertilizer for cacti and succulents ◊ When dry. Water sparingly in winter ▥ Tip or leaf cuttings

△ *Crassula perforata*
**STRING OF BUTTONS**
↕ ↔ 30cm (12in)

A curiosity for a sunny spot. Erect stems pass through the middle of the paired, green, succulent leaves. Scented, starry, white to pink flowers appear in summer.

☼ Bright, with some sun ❚ Warm, but cool to moderate in winter. Low humidity ◕ Monthly, using fertilizer for cacti and succulents ◊ When dry. Water sparingly in winter ▥ Tip or leaf cuttings

**OTHER HOUSEPLANTS WITH UNUSUAL FOLIAGE**

*Asplenium bulbiferum*
*Beaucarnea recurvata*, see p.96
*Begonia lubbersii*
*Cryptanthus zonatus*
*Cycas revoluta*, see p.96
*Dionaea muscipula*, see p.118
*Fascicularia bicolor*
*Passiflora coriacea*
*Pseudopanax ferox*
*Tolmiea menziesii*, see p.67

△ *Euphorbia trigona* 'Purpurea'
**AFRICAN MILK TREE**
↕ 1.5m (5ft) ↔ 1m (3ft)

This purple-tinted form of a succulent spurge is from Namibia. Sitting bolt upright, it has three-angled stems lined with leaves that fall at the end of summer.

☼ Bright ❚ Warm, but cool to moderate in winter. Low humidity ◕ Monthly, using fertilizer for cacti and succulents ◊ When compost surface dry. Water sparingly in winter ▥ Stem cuttings

△ *Faucaria tigrina*
**TIGER JAWS**
↕ 10cm (4in) ↔ 20cm (8in)

Most small children will be fascinated by this plant – the leaves resemble those of a succulent Venus fly trap, but with sharp teeth. The yellow flowers, borne in autumn, are a pleasant surprise.

☼ Bright, with some sun ❚ Warm, but cool to moderate in winter. Low humidity ◕ Monthly, using fertilizer for cacti and succulents ◊ When dry. Water sparingly in winter ▥ Stem or leaf cuttings

**OTHER SUCCULENT HOUSE-PLANTS WITH UNUSUAL FOLIAGE**

*Haworthia attenuata* f. *clariperla*
*Pachyphytum oviferum*, see p.111
*Sedum pachyphyllum*
*Senecio rowleyanus*, see p.93
*Titanopsis calcarea*

△ *Tillandsia caput-medusae*
**AIR PLANT**
↕ 40cm (16in) ↔ 24cm (10in)

Curved and twisted, horn-like leaves grow from a bulbous base that can be attached to a piece of hanging cork or driftwood. Blue and red flower spikes show in spring.

☼ Bright, but avoid direct sun ❚ Warm. Low to moderate humidity ◕ Every eight weeks ◊ Mist daily. Mist four times a week in low light and at low temperatures ▥ Offsets

**FOLIAGE EFFECT**

# LOCATIONS

TEMPERATURE, HUMIDITY, and light determine the environment in any location, and therefore which plants will grow well there. Before choosing a houseplant to suit a particular spot, you should also consider the size of the room, how often it is used, and for what type of activity.

△ SUNNY SITTING ROOM *Glass doors, white walls, and a mirror make the most of all the natural light available, encouraging flowering plants to bloom.*

*Celosia argentea* 'Plumosa' for sunny windowsills

Remember that indoor "climates" are affected by seasonal changes outside. Increased central heating can make the air very dry in winter, and light levels will generally be greater in summer. You may need to move your plants as the seasons change to keep them healthy.

### LIGHT AND HEAT
The number and size of windows in any location will determine the level of natural light. Full light through glass, but not hot summer sun, is appreciated by the majority of plants, particularly those that flower. Poorly-lit corners, where nothing seems to flourish, are more challenging, but can be enlivened by a range of shade-tolerant plants.

Plants that enjoy high heat and humidity, such as tropical species, may not seem to have a place in the home, but many are extremely adaptable and will accept lower temperatures or a drier atmosphere for limited periods. You can also use a pebble tray to raise humidity. Equally adaptable are houseplants that tolerate low light, cool temperatures, or dry air; they will often grow where no others survive.

### CHANGING ROOMS
There are few rooms in any home that cannot be improved by a plant. The principal rooms – sitting and dining rooms, bedrooms, studies, bathrooms, and kitchens – can be "decorated" with a great variety of species. Garden rooms and conservatories can support the widest range of plants, depending on their heat and humidity levels, but don't give up on small areas like halls, landings, or washrooms – they can often support at least one plant.

△ OFFICE WINNER *Compact, easy to care for, and tolerant of neglect, this pilea is a good choice for a busy home office.*

◁ LOW-LIGHT KITCHEN *An impressive nephrolepis thrives in this warm kitchen, where light levels are usually low.*

▷ HUMID BATHROOM *Many ferns will appreciate the often damp atmosphere of a warm bathroom, if it is not too bright.*

# Houseplants for Sunny Windowsills

A SUNNY WINDOWSILL, its heat magnified by the glass, can be the hottest spot in the house, where only a few plants other than cacti and succulents will survive for long without scorching. However, a host of plants enjoy such a position if they are protected from the excessive heat of midday in summer; draw blinds or curtains or just move them out of the way.

*Ananas bracteatus* 'Tricolor' ▷
**VARIEGATED WILD PINEAPPLE**
↕ 70cm (28in) ↔ 50cm (20in)

Striking in foliage and flower, but beware of the viciously spine-toothed leaves. The impressive pineapple flowerhead appears in summer. Needs regular watering.

☼ Bright, with some sun ♨ Warm. Moderate to high humidity ◑ Fortnightly, using flowering houseplant fertilizer ◊ When compost surface just dry ▭ Offsets, rosettes

△ *Celosia argentea* 'Plumosa'
**CELOSIA, PLUME FLOWER**
↕ ↔ 45cm (18in)

This striking perennial, normally grown as an annual, needs plenty of light. Protect it from midday sun to prolong the richly-coloured, plumed summer flowerhead.

☼ Bright, but avoid hot summer sun ♨ Moderate to warm. Moderate humidity ◑ Fortnightly ◊ Water when compost surface just dry ▭ Seed. Germinates very freely

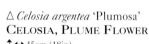

---

**OTHER HOUSEPLANTS FOR SUNNY WINDOWSILLS**

*Cyrtanthus elatus*
*Nerium oleander* cultivars
*Pelargonium* 'Graveolens', see p.46
*Pentas lanceolata*
*Plumeria rubra*
*Punica granatum* var. *nana*

---

*Bougainvillea* 'Dania' ▷
**BOUGAINVILLEA, PAPER FLOWER**
↕ ↔ 1m (3ft) or more

Brilliant, bright pink bracts are borne from summer to autumn. This exotic-looking plant can be bought young, trained to a framework, and pruned to control its size, but it will grow larger if given the space.

☼ Bright, with sun ♨ Moderate to warm. Low humidity ◑ Fortnightly, using flowering houseplant fertilizer ◊ When compost surface just dry. Water sparingly in winter ▭ Tip cuttings

*Browallia speciosa* 'White Troll' ▷
**SAPPHIRE FLOWER**
↕ ↔ 25cm (10in)

Perennial but usually grown as an annual, the sapphire flower has pointed leaves that are slightly clammy to the touch and produces white summer flowers. Pinch out the tips to encourage a bushy habit.

☼ Bright to moderate, avoiding hot summer sun ♨ Cool to moderate. Moderate humidity ◑ Fortnightly feed ◊ Water when compost surface dry ▭ Seed

△ *Crassula socialis*
**CRASSULA**
↕ 7cm (3in) ↔ 30cm (12in)

Small, dense rosettes of horny-margined leaves soon form colonies, with heads of miniature, star-shaped white flowers produced in spring. A reliable houseplant.

☼ Bright, with some sun ☷ Warm, but cool to moderate in winter. Low humidity ◢ Monthly, using fertilizer for cacti and succulents ◌ When dry. Water sparingly in winter ☷ Tip or leaf cuttings

**OTHER SUCCULENT HOUSE-PLANTS FOR SUNNY WINDOWSILLS**

*Anacampseros alstonii*
*Crassula perfoliata* var. *minor*
*Euphorbia caput-medusae*
*Lampranthus purpureus*
*Portulacaria afra* 'Foliis-variegatus'
*Pterodiscus speciosus*

△ *Huernia thuretii* var. *primulina*
**CARRION FLOWER, HUERNIA**
↕ ↔ 8cm (3in)

A clump-forming succulent with sharp-angled, grey-green stems, bearing curious, creamy-yellow, red-freckled flowers in summer and autumn. Do not overwater.

☼ Bright, with sun ☷ Warm, but cool to moderate in winter. Low humidity ◢ Monthly, using fertilizer for cacti and succulents ◌ When compost surface dry. Water sparingly in winter ☷ Tip cuttings

△ *Parodia leninghausii*
**GOLDEN BALL CACTUS**
↕ 60cm (2ft) ↔ 8cm (3in)

Initially ball-shaped or rounded, this cactus later develops into a fat, golden-spined column. Pale yellow flowers are produced from the tips in summer.

☼ Bright, with sun ☷ Warm, but cool to moderate in winter. Low humidity ◢ Monthly, using fertilizer for cacti and succulents ◌ When compost surface dry. Water sparingly in winter ☷ Tip cuttings

**LOCATIONS**

△ *Hibiscus rosa-sinensis* 'Scarlet Giant'
**CHINESE HIBISCUS,
ROSE OF CHINA**
↕ 2m (6ft) or more ↔ 1.5m (5ft) or more

A large plant, but careful pruning controls its size. It loves sun, which encourages free flowering from spring to autumn; the red blooms can be up to 17cm (7in) across.

☼ Bright, with sun ☷ Warm, avoiding fluctuation. Moderate to high humidity ◢ Fortnightly. Stop in cool conditions ◌ When just dry. Water sparingly in winter. Avoid waterlogging ☷ Semi-ripe cuttings

*Richly coloured leaves*

◁ *Solenostemon* 'Defiance'
**COLEUS,
FLAME NETTLE**
↕ ↔ 30cm (12in)

Bright green and claret foliage distinguishes this coleus. Many selections are available. Although perennial, these soft-stemmed plants are generally treated as annuals; pinch out tips for bushiness.

☼ Bright, with sun ☷ Warm. Low humidity ◢ Weekly. Occasionally in winter ◌ Keep moist, but avoid waterlogging. In winter, water when just dry ☷ Tip cuttings. Roots easily in water

# Houseplants for Full Light

A SITUATION IN FULL LIGHT, as long as there is no risk
of scorching or overheating, is ideal for many houseplants. The best-lit spots in any house are
usually on or near windowsills that receive
plenty of daylight; this could even be early morning or
late evening sun. However, all the plants featured here will
need protection from strong midday sun in summer.

*Capsicum annuum*
'Carnival Red' ▷
ORNAMENTAL
PEPPER
↕ ↔ 60cm (2ft)

A familiar plant, usually
treated as an annual, but
longer-lasting given cool
conditions. In winter, the
freely-borne, brilliant
orange-red fruits stud
the leafy branches.

☼ Bright ❄ Cool to
moderate. Moderate
humidity ♦ Fortnightly,
alternating general fertilizer
with flowering houseplant
fertilizer ♦ When just dry
✂ Tip cuttings

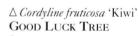

△ *Cordyline fruticosa* 'Kiwi'
GOOD LUCK TREE
↕ ↔ 2m (6ft)

This suckering plant forms a clump of
erect stems clothed in bold foliage that is
striped dark green, pale green, and cream,
and has subtly pink-tinted margins.

☼ Bright, but avoid summer sun ❄ Warm. High
humidity ♦ Fortnightly. Monthly in winter ♦ When
compost surface dry. Reduce watering at lower
temperatures ✂ Tip cuttings, stem sections

---

### OTHER HOUSEPLANTS FOR FULL LIGHT WITH SOME SUMMER SUN

*Capsicum annuum*, see p.98
*Correa* 'Dusky Bells'
*Crassula coccinea*
*Cyrtanthus elatus*
*Fuchsia* 'Ballet Girl'
*Gloriosa superba* 'Rothschildiana'
*Heterocentron elegans*
*Impatiens walleriana* hybrids, see p.87
*Kalanchoe* 'Wendy'

---

△ *Chrysanthemum indicum*
FLORISTS' CHRYSANTHEMUM
↕ ↔ 30cm (12in)

A dwarf form with a compact habit and
pale yellow flowers, borne from autumn to
winter. A valuable temporary plant and
one of many popular chrysanthemums.

☼ Bright, but avoid direct sun ❄ Cool to
moderate. Moderate humidity ♦ Every three weeks
♦ Keep moist, but avoid waterlogging ✂ Tip
cuttings

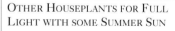

◁ *Crassula arborescens*
SILVER JADE PLANT
↕ 2m (6ft) ↔ 1.2m (4ft)

Slow-growing but eventually substantial,
this succulent shrub bears striking, red-
margined, grey-green leaves, and white
starry flowers from autumn to winter.

☼ Bright, with some sun ❄ Warm, but cool to
moderate in winter. Low humidity ♦ Monthly, using
fertilizer for cacti and succulents ♦ When dry.
Water sparingly in winter ✂ Stem or leaf cuttings

*Justicia brandegeeana* ▷
**SHRIMP PLANT**
↕ ↔ 90cm (3ft)

Free- and long-flowering, this popular plant has colourful bracts and pendent white flowers, borne throughout the year. It likes some sun. Previously called *Beloperone guttata*. ▽

☼ Bright to moderate, avoiding hottest sun ▮ Warm, avoiding draughts. Moderate to high humidity ▮ Monthly ▮ Keep moist, but avoid waterlogging ▮ Tip cuttings

△ *Dudleya pulverulenta*
**DUDLEYA**
↕ ↔ 30cm (12in) or more

Red or yellow starry flowers, produced in spring or early summer, complement this succulent's rosette of fleshy, pointed, silvery grey leaves, borne on a short stem.

☼ Bright, with sun ▮ Warm, but cool to moderate in winter. Low humidity ▮ Monthly, using cactus and succulent fertilizer ▮ When compost surface dry. Water sparingly in winter ▮ Stem or leaf cuttings

◁ *Smithiantha* 'Orange King'
**TEMPLE BELLS**
↕ ↔ 30cm (12in)

Beautifully mottled, densely hairy leaves appear in spring after a winter dormancy, topped from summer to autumn by loose heads of pendulous orange flowers.

☼ Bright to moderate. Avoid hot sun ▮ Warm, but moderate in dormancy. High humidity ▮ Fortnightly, using flowering houseplant fertilizer ▮ Keep moist, increasing in growth. Stop in dormancy ▮ Division

OTHER HOUSEPLANTS FOR
FULL LIGHT AWAY FROM
SUMMER SUN

*Achimenes* hybrids
*Aeschynanthus lobbianus*
*Aphelandra*
  *squarrosa* 'Dania',
  see p.70
*Justicia rizzinii*, see p.33
*Mandevilla rosea*
*Pachystachys lutea*
*Schlumbergera*
  *truncata*, see p.65
*Thunbergia alata*, see p.95

*Hoya carnosa* 'Variegata' ▷
**WAX PLANT**
↕ ↔ 2m (6ft)

Capable of great vigour, this handsome, creamy-variegated form of the twining wax plant can be trained on a frame to keep it neat and manageable. The fragrant, waxy flowers appear in summer.

☼ Bright, but avoid direct sun ▮ Moderate to warm. Moderate to high humidity ▮ Every three weeks, using flowering houseplant fertilizer ▮ Water when compost surface dry. Avoid overwatering ▮ Tip cuttings

△ *Streptocarpus* 'Kim'
**CAPE PRIMROSE**
↕ 20cm (8in) ↔ 35cm (14in)

This Cape primrose produces rosettes of downy leaves, and branching sprays of dark purple, white-eyed summer flowers. A classic houseplant for a well-lit spot. ▽

☼ Bright to moderate. Avoid direct sun ▮ Warm. Moderate to high humidity ▮ Flowering houseplant fertilizer fortnightly. Monthly in winter, unless dormant ▮ When dry ▮ Division, leaf cuttings

# Houseplants for Medium Light

MOST ROOMS HAVE an area of medium light, out of direct sunlight but not in shade. It is usually a few metres from a window, or closer if you have sheer curtains or blinds. All the plants here tolerate medium light, but will benefit from a short spell in full light.

LOCATIONS

*Aglaonema* 'Marie' ▷
**PAINTED DROP TONGUE**
↕ 1.2m (4ft) ↔ 60cm (2ft)

Aglaonemas, noted for their subtle leaf patterns, include this bushy form with large, dark green foliage splashed grey-green. A fine specimen houseplant.

☼ Bright to moderate ▮ Moderate to warm, avoiding fluctuation. Moderate humidity ♦ Foliage houseplant fertilizer weekly. Monthly in winter ◊ When dry ▦ Division, tip cuttings, stem sections

△ *Begonia* 'Tiger Paws'
**EYELASH BEGONIA**
↕ 20cm (8in) ↔ 25cm (10in)

An eye-catching houseplant that forms a compact mound of shield-like, lime-green leaves, marked and edged bronze, each with a curious fringe of "eyelash" hairs.

☼ Bright to moderate ▮ Cool to warm. Moderate humidity ♦ Fortnightly. Monthly in winter ◊ Water when compost surface just dry ▦ Division, leaf cuttings

△ *Dracaena cincta* 'Bicolor'
**DRACAENA**
↕ 4m (12ft) ↔ 1m (3ft)

This is one of several variegated forms of *Dracaena cincta*, with cream-edged leaves. Perfect for a semi-shady corner or hallway, or as an architectural feature plant.

☼ Bright to moderate ▮ Moderate to warm. Moderate to high humidity ♦ Fortnightly. Occasionally during winter ◊ Water when compost surface dry ▦ Tip cuttings, stem sections

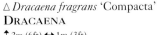

△ *Dracaena fragrans* 'Compacta'
**DRACAENA**
↕ 2m (6ft) ↔ 1m (3ft)

Masses of dark green leaves top the stems of these robust plants, making them look like shaving brushes. Cut mature plants back hard in spring to promote regrowth.

☼ Bright to moderate. Growth stops in low light ▮ Moderate to warm. Moderate to high humidity ♦ Fortnightly. Occasionally in winter ◊ When compost surface dry ▦ Tip cuttings, stem sections

---

**OTHER LARGE HOUSEPLANTS FOR MEDIUM LIGHT**

*Aspidistra elatior* 'Milky Way', see p.66
*Asplenium nidus*, see p.108
*Chamaedorea elegans*, see p.114
*Dracaena marginata*, see p.97
*Fatsia japonica*, see p.41
*Monstera deliciosa*, see p.41
*Nephrolepis exaltata* 'Bostoniensis', see p.109
*Philodendron* 'Medisa', see p.95

△ *Ficus pumila* 'White Sonny'
**CREEPING FIG**

↕ ↔ 30cm (12in) or more

The tiny leaves of this creeping fig are edged with a bold cream line. In humid conditions, it produces climbing roots and will grow happily up a suitable support.

☼ Bright to moderate ≣ Moderate to warm. Moderate to high humidity ◊ Fortnightly, using foliage houseplant fertilizer. Occasionally in winter ◊ When dry, especially if cool 🏶 Tip cuttings

---

### OTHER SMALL HOUSEPLANTS FOR MEDIUM LIGHT

*Adiantum raddianum* 'Fritz Luth', see p.82
*Aglaonema* 'Lilian', see p.76
*Cyrtomium falcatum*
*Hedera helix* 'Très Coupé'
*Plectranthus australis*
*Saxifraga stolonifera*, see p.93
*Schlumbergera* × *buckleyi*
*Tolmiea menziesii* 'Taff's Gold', see p.79

---

△ *Hedera helix* 'California'
**COMMON IVY, ENGLISH IVY**

↕ 1m (3ft) ↔ 30cm (12in)

The attractive, mid-green leaves of this ivy vary from triangular to broadly heart-shaped. It is ideal for growing in a hanging basket or for climbing up a support.

☼ Bright to moderate. Poor growth in low light ≣ Cool to moderate. Moderate to high humidity ◊ Fortnightly. Twice in winter ◊ When dry. Water sparingly in winter 🏶 Tip cuttings, layering

*Schlumbergera truncata* △
**CRAB CACTUS**

↕ 30cm (12in) ↔ 60cm (2ft)

From late autumn to winter, pendent, deep pink flowers cover this bold cactus, which then has a rest period. Succulent, flattened, segmented stems add interest.

☼ Moderate ≣ Moderate to warm, but cool when resting. Moderate humidity ◊ Fortnightly in growth, using high potash fertilizer ◊ Keep moist in growth. Water sparingly during rest period 🏶 Stem sections

LOCATIONS

△ *Fittonia verschaffeltii* 'Janita'
**NET PLANT, SNAKESKIN PLANT**

↕ 15cm (6in) ↔ 30cm (12in) or more

Display this small, dense, creeping net plant on a low surface to appreciate its beautiful pink-netted green leaves. Ideal for terraria or warm, humid bathrooms.

☼ Moderate ≣ Moderate to warm. High humidity ◊ Fortnightly. Occasionally in winter ◊ Water when compost surface just dry. Avoid waterlogging 🏶 Tip cuttings

*Philodendron erubescens* 'Red Emerald' ▷
**BLUSHING PHILODENDRON**

↕ 5m (15ft) ↔ 2m (6ft) or more

This stunning form of a vigorous rainforest climber has glossy, emerald-green leaves and dark red main stems and leaf stalks. Best trained up a moss pole.

☼ Bright to shady ≣ Moderate to warm. Moderate to high humidity ◊ Fortnightly, using foliage houseplant fertilizer. Monthly in winter ◊ Water when compost surface dry 🏶 Tip cuttings

65

# Houseplants for Low Light

HOUSEPLANTS THAT THRIVE in low light are a small but resilient group; of course, those featured here will all benefit from a little extra attention to help them look their best. Low-lit areas are typically those furthest from a window or other source of light; however, they do not include dark, dingy corners, where any plant will face a struggle to survive.

LOCATIONS

△ *Fittonia* 'Bianco Verde'
**SILVER NET LEAF**
↕ 15cm (6in) ↔ 30cm (12in)

Small, variegated leaves and a creeping habit make this fittonia an excellent terrarium plant. It thrives in low light, provided that conditions are suitably warm and moist; group several on a pebble tray to raise humidity.

☼ Moderate to shady, avoiding direct sun ⬛ Warm. High humidity ◑ Fortnightly. Occasionally in winter ◐ Keep moist, but avoid waterlogging ⬛ Tip cuttings

*Aspidistra elatior* 'Milky Way' ▷
**ASPIDISTRA, CAST IRON PLANT**
↕ ↔ 60cm (2ft)

Few plants tolerate poor light levels better than the cast iron plant. It is almost impervious to neglect, but naturally responds well to generous treatment. This spotted form is particularly ornamental; a fine specimen plant.

☼ Moderate to shady. Direct sun will scorch leaves ⬛ Moderate to warm. Moderate humidity ◑ Every three weeks ◐ When compost surface dry. Dislikes waterlogging ⬛ Division, offsets

*Deeply-lobed mature leaf*

△ *Duchesnea indica*
**MOCK STRAWBERRY**
↕ 10cm (4in) ↔ 1.2m (4ft)

A fast-creeping perennial that forms a carpet of runners covered with strawberry-like leaves. Yellow flowers are produced in summer, but to obtain the red fruits, move it to a brighter position.

☼ Moderate to shady ⬛ Cool to moderate. Moderate to high humidity ◑ Every three weeks ◐ Keep moist. Reduce watering during winter ⬛ Plantlets

◁ *Philodendron bipinnatifidum*
**TREE PHILODENDRON**
↕ 3m (10ft) ↔ 2m (6ft) or more

One of the most spectacular foliage plants, with its strong stems and large, deeply lobed, long-stalked mature leaves (see inset). Grow this Brazilian shrub on a stout moss pole or frame. ♈

☼ Bright to shady ⬛ Warm. Moderate to high humidity ◑ Fortnightly, using foliage houseplant fertilizer ◐ Water when compost surface slightly dry ⬛ Division, tip cuttings

*Philodendron scandens* ▷
## HEART LEAF, SWEETHEART PLANT
↕ ↔ 3m (10ft)

Vigorous and, given the space, high climbing, this superb plant has deep glossy green, heart-shaped, slender-pointed leaves that can reach up to 30cm (12in) long. It makes an unusual and impressive sight in a hanging basket, or grow it on a moss pole or frame.

☼ Bright to shady ⬛ Moderate to warm. Moderate to high humidity ◑ Fortnightly, using foliage houseplant fertilizer. Monthly in winter ◒ Let the compost surface dry slightly before watering ⬚ Tip cuttings

△ *Soleirolia soleirolii*
## MIND-YOUR-OWN-BUSINESS
↕ 5cm (2in) ↔ 30cm (12in)

Resembling a moss because of its low, carpeting growth and tiny leaves, this plant makes close ground cover for pots or hanging baskets. Not suitable for terraria.

☼ Bright to shady, avoiding direct sun ⬛ Cool to moderate. Moderate to high humidity ◑ Every three weeks. Rarely in winter ◒ Keep moist, but avoid waterlogging. Sparingly in winter ⬚ Division

△ *Selaginella martensii*
## SELAGINELLA
↕ 15cm (6in) ↔ 30cm (12in)

A curious, tufted fern relative with flattened, frond-like stems, crowded with small, scale-like, glossy green leaves that give the plant a pleasantly soft texture. Makes good cover beneath other plants.

☼ Shady ⬛ Warm. High humidity ◑ Every five weeks, using half-strength general houseplant fertilizer ◒ Water when compost surface just dry ⬚ Stem cuttings

△ *Tolmiea menziesii*
## PIGGYBACK PLANT
↕ 30cm (12in) ↔ 40cm (16in)

This hardy perennial produces young plantlets where the leaf blades join their stalks. Suitable for an unheated room, it looks good in a pot or hanging basket.

☼ Moderate to shady ⬛ Cool to moderate. Moderate humidity ◑ Fortnightly. Occasionally in winter ◒ When compost surface dry. Reduce watering in winter ⬚ Division, plantlets

△ *Schefflera arboricola* 'Luciana'
## SCHEFFLERA
↕ 1.8m (6ft) ↔ 90cm (3ft)

Fingered leaves are the hallmark of these evergreen shrubs from Taiwan, which all make excellent houseplants. They branch from the base, so prune to keep small.

☼ Bright to shady ⬛ Warm, avoiding fluctuation. Moderate to high humidity ◑◑ Fortnightly. Monthly in winter ◒ Water when compost surface dry ⬚ Tip cuttings, air layering

### OTHER HOUSEPLANTS FOR LOW LIGHT

*Adiantum raddianum*, see p.100
*Aucuba japonica* 'Crotonifolia'
*Chamaedorea elegans*, see p.114
*Ficus pumila* 'White Sonny', see p.65
*Hedera canariensis* 'Gloire de Marengo'
*Howea forsteriana*
*Spathiphyllum* 'Euro Gigant', see p.73
*Tolmiea menziesii* 'Taff's Gold', see p.79

# Houseplants for Dry Atmospheres

$C$ENTRAL HEATING has both benefits and drawbacks for houseplants. It keeps a room warm, which suits most exotics, but it also causes moisture in the air to evaporate, leaving the room very dry. Regular misting counteracts this, or choose from the range of plants that are tolerant of, if not comfortable in, a dry atmosphere.

L O C A T I O N S

*Adenium obesum* ▷
**DESERT ROSE**
↕ 1.5m (5ft) ↔ 1m (3ft)

A slow-growing succulent bush that develops a swollen base. Red, pink, or white flowers appear from midwinter to spring, usually before the leaves; the early flowers are often a surprise.

☼ Bright, with sun ◢ Warm, but moderate to cool winter rest. Low humidity ◐ Every three weeks, using cactus and succulent or high potash fertilizer ◊ When top 2.5cm (1in) compost dry. Water sparingly in winter ▨ Tip cuttings

△ *Aloe aristata*
**LACE ALOE**
↕ 12cm (5in) ↔ 30cm (12in)

Crowded rosettes of spine-tipped leaves are minutely white-toothed and spotted; the orange-red flowers appear in autumn. Easy to grow and very tolerant of neglect.

☼ Bright, with sun ◢ Warm, but moderate to cool in winter. Low humidity ◐ Every three weeks, using fertilizer for cacti and succulents ◊ When top 2.5cm (1in) compost dry. Sparingly in winter ▨ Offsets

**OTHER HOUSEPLANTS FOR DRY ATMOSPHERES**

*Azorina vidalii*
*Beaucarnea recurvata*, see p.96
*Bowiea volubilis*
*Haemanthus albiflos*
*Pelargonium* 'Graveolens', see p.46
*Sedum sieboldii* 'Mediovariegatum'

△ *Astrophytum myriostigma*
**BISHOP'S CAP**
↕ 23cm (9in) ↔ 25cm (10in)

Spiny when young, and later smooth, this squat, plump-ribbed cactus is covered in minute, white-downy scales. Pale yellow summer flowers grow from the crown. ♈

☼ Bright, with sun ◢ Warm, but cool to moderate in winter. Low humidity ◐ Monthly, using fertilizer for cacti and succulents ◊ When compost surface dry. Water sparingly in winter ▨ Offsets, seed

*Aechmea chantinii* ▷
**QUEEN OF THE AECHMEAS**
↕ 1m (3ft) ↔ 80cm (32in)

As long as the urn-like rosette is topped up, this impressive, red- and yellow-bracted bromeliad tolerates a reasonably dry atmosphere, although it appreciates misting. ♈

☼ Bright, but avoid summer sun ◢ Warm. Low to moderate humidity ◐ Fortnightly ◊ When compost surface dry. Water sparingly in winter. Keep "urn" topped up with water ▨ Offsets

△ *Euphorbia obesa*
**TURKISH TEMPLE**
↕ ↔ 15cm (6in)

This plant looks like an *Astrophytum*, but it is in fact a succulent spurge, with typically milky caustic sap. The small yellow flower clusters are produced in summer.

☼ Bright, with sun ▤ Warm, but cool to moderate in winter. Low humidity ◌ Monthly, using fertilizer for cacti and succulents ◌ When compost surface dry. Water sparingly in winter ▱ Offsets

*Vibrant orange flowerhead*

△ *Opuntia microdasys* var. *albispina*
**BUNNY EARS**
↕ ↔ 60cm (2ft)

A very decorative cactus producing bright yellow flowers in spring and summer. Handle with care; minute white spines stick into skin at the slightest touch.

☼ Bright, with sun ▤ Warm, but cool to moderate in winter. Low humidity ◌ Monthly, using cactus and succulent fertilizer ◌ When compost surface dry. Sparingly in winter ▱ Offsets

△ *Tillandsia deiriana*
**AIR PLANT**
↕ ↔ 30cm (12in)

This vibrantly-coloured air plant is best grown on a piece of driftwood or cork and suspended from a high point that is reachable for misting. It can also be pot grown.

☼ Bright, but avoid direct sun ▤ Warm. Low humidity ◌ Every eight weeks ◌ Mist daily. Mist four times weekly in low light and cool conditions. Water sparingly ▱ Offsets

---

**OTHER CACTI AND SUCCULENTS FOR DRY ATMOSPHERES**

*Agave victoriae-reginae*
*Aloe variegata*, see p.88
*Kalanchoe daigremontiana*
*Mammillaria hahniana*
*Opuntia tunicata*
*Oreocereus celsianus*
*Pedilanthus tithymaloides* 'Variegatus'

---

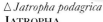

△ *Jatropha podagrica*
**JATROPHA**
↕ 50cm (20in) or more ↔ 25cm (10in) or more

Swollen stems bear large, tough, long-stalked leaves, whitish beneath. Clusters of red flowers appear at the ends of long stalks in summer. It has caustic sap.

☼ Bright, with sun ▤ Warm, but cool to moderate in winter. Low humidity ◌ Monthly, using fertilizer for cacti and succulents ◌ When compost surface dry. Water sparingly in winter ▱ Seed

*Grey, curled foliage*

◁ *Tillandsia streptophylla*
**AIR PLANT**
↕ ↔ 45cm (18in)

Striking, curled and arching foliage is joined in late spring or autumn by green bracts and blue and red flowers. Grow in a pot or display on a piece of driftwood.

☼ Bright, but avoid direct sun ▤ Warm. Low humidity ◌ Every eight weeks ◌ Mist daily. Mist four times weekly in low light and cool conditions. Water sparingly ▱ Offsets

# Houseplants for Warm, Humid Rooms

A WARM, HUMID ENVIRONMENT is perfect for growing many tropical plants, but remember that some need constant moderate to high humidity to flourish, disliking draughts and changes in temperature. Warm bathrooms are a good choice, but beware of open windows letting in unwelcome cold air, and the drying effect of heating. Garden rooms, with controlled temperature and humidity, are ideal, and enable you to nurture exotics or a miniature rainforest.

LOCATIONS

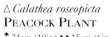

*Aphelandra squarrosa* 'Dania' ▷
**ZEBRA PLANT**
↕ ↔ 30cm (12in)

Grow this compact plant for its dark green glossy leaves with their creamy veins and midribs, and its eye-catching flowers with their bright yellow, orange-tipped bracts.

☼ Bright to moderate, avoiding hot sun ▮ Warm, avoiding fluctuation. High humidity ◓ Fortnightly, spring to autumn ◊ Keep moist, but do not over-water. When dry in winter ▦ Tip cuttings

△ *Calathea roseopicta*
**PEACOCK PLANT**
↕ 24cm (10in) ↔ 15cm (6in)

A distinctive plant bearing beautifully patterned, large foliage, marked with deep green; the midrib and leaf margins are a delicate rose-pink. A stunning houseplant.

☼ Moderate ▮ Moderate to warm, avoiding fluctuation. High humidity ◓ Fortnightly. Monthly in winter ◊ Keep moist. At cooler temperatures, water when compost surface just dry ▦ Division

△ *Caladium bicolor* 'Frieda Hemple'
**ANGEL'S WINGS**
↕ 30cm (12in) ↔ 45cm (18in)

Gloriously coloured, paper-thin leaves emerge in spring and die down in autumn, when the tubers should be lifted and stored for replanting the following spring.

☼ Bright to moderate, avoiding direct sun ▮ Warm, but moderate in dormancy. High humidity ◓ Weekly ◊ Keep moist, reduce in autumn, and keep slightly moist in winter ▦ Division, tubers

△ *Calathea makoyana*
**PEACOCK PLANT**
↕ 45cm (18in) ↔ 30cm (12in)

Also known as cathedral windows, this elegant plant has large, oval, mid-green leaves, beautifully traced with darker green and flushed purple beneath. ♔

☼ Moderate ▮ Moderate to warm, avoiding fluctuation. High humidity ◓ Fortnightly. Monthly in winter ◊ Keep moist. At cooler temperatures, water when compost surface just dry ▦ Division

△ *Codiaeum variegatum* var. *pictum*
**CROTON, JOSEPH'S COAT**
↕ 2m (6ft) ↔ 1.2m (4ft)

This woody-based plant is famous for the colourful variegation along the veins of its glossy leaves. Green and yellow, or red, orange, and purple are predominant.

☼ Bright, but avoid summer sun ▮ Moderate to warm, avoiding fluctuation. High humidity ◓ Fortnightly in summer, using foliage houseplant fertilizer ◊ Keep moist. When dry if cool ▦ Tip cuttings

*Maranta leuconeura*
var. *kerchoveana* ▷
**PRAYER PLANT**
↕ ↔ 30cm (12in)

Pale green, satin-sheened leaves, each marked with dark green "footprints", distinguish this tropical American species and give it its alternative name, rabbit's foot plant. 🏆

△ *Cyperus albostriatus*
**UMBRELLA PLANT**
↕ 60cm (2ft) ↔ 30cm (12in)

Densely tufted and with strap-shaped, pale green leaves radiating from the ends of the stems, this plant also produces green flower clusters from summer to autumn.

☼ Bright to moderate. Avoid summer sun ▮ Cool to warm. Moderate to high humidity ♦ Fortnightly, using foliage houseplant fertilizer. Twice in winter ♦ Keep moist. Likes to stand in water ▧ Division

**OTHER HOUSEPLANTS FOR WARM, HUMID ROOMS**

*Adiantum raddianum* 'Gracillimum'
*Anthurium crystallinum*, see p.40
*Calathea crocata*, see p.30
*Codiaeum* 'Petra'
*Hypoestes phyllostachya* 'Wit', see p.53
*Maranta leuconeura* var.
  *erythroneura*, see p.101
*Peperomia caperata* 'Little
  Fantasy'
*Philodendron melanochrysum*
*Sinningia* 'Mont Blanc', see p.45

☼ Moderate, avoiding direct sun ▮ Moderate to warm. High humidity ♦ Fortnightly. Occasionally in winter ♦ Keep moist. When dry at lower temperatures ▧ Division, tip cuttings

L O C A T I O N S

△ *Fittonia verschaffeltii* var. *pearcei*
'Superba Red'
**NET PLANT, SNAKESKIN PLANT**
↕ 15cm (6in) ↔ 30cm (12in) or more

A compact plant with dark green leaves and bright red leaf veins. It makes a neat display when grouped with several others in a shallow pot, or is ideal for a terrarium.

☼ Moderate ▮ Moderate to warm. High humidity ♦ Fortnightly. Occasionally in winter ♦ Allow compost surface to dry slightly before watering. Dislikes being waterlogged ▧ Tip cuttings

*Stromanthe* 'Stripestar' ▷
**PEACOCK PLANT**
↕ 1.5m (5ft) ↔ 1m (3ft)

Each glossy dark green leaf has a pale green midrib and veins, with a dark purple underside that is prominent as new leaves unfurl. Not easy to grow but worth the effort.

☼ Bright to moderate, avoiding summer sun ▮ Moderate to warm, avoiding draughts. High humidity ♦ Fortnightly. Monthly in winter ♦ Keep moist. When dry at lower temperatures ▧ Division

# Houseplants for Large Rooms

OTHER HOUSEPLANTS FOR LARGE ROOMS

*Begonia luxurians*
*Chamaedorea elegans*, see p.114
*Cissus rhombifolia* 'Ellen Danica', see p.78
*Ficus elastica* 'Robusta', see p.91
*Ficus lyrata*, see p.97
*Musa acuminata* 'Dwarf Cavendish'
*Sparrmannia africana*, see p.89
*Yucca elephantipes*, see p.87

G ENEROUSLY-PROPORTIONED rooms call for dramatic plants to fill the space without dominating it or making it hard for people to move around. Bold-leaved specimens are often a good choice, although large plants with smaller leaves are equally effective when well placed. Some of the suggestions here need careful pruning to restrict their size.

### *Fatsia japonica* 'Variegata' ▷
### JAPANESE ARALIA
↕ ↔ 1.5m (5ft) or more

A popular variegated foliage shrub, with large, long-stalked, evergreen leaves, their lobes splashed creamy-white. Tolerates relatively cool conditions, but it needs plenty of elbow room. 🏆

☼ Bright to moderate 🌡 Cool to moderate. Moderate humidity 💧 Fortnightly, using foliage houseplant fertilizer. Once in winter 💧 When compost surface dry. Reduce watering at low temperatures 🌱 Tip cuttings, air layering

△ *Codiaeum* 'Juliet'
### CROTON
↕ ↔ 1m (3ft) or more

This handsome evergreen shrub has deeply-lobed, leathery, glossy green leaves, their veins picked out in bright yellow. Plant several in a container, or encourage one to branch out.

☼ Bright, with some sun 🌡 Warm, avoiding draughts and fluctuation. Moderate to high humidity 💧 Fortnightly, using foliage houseplant fertilizer. Occasionally in winter 💧 Keep moist. In winter, water when compost surface dry 🌱 Tip cuttings

*Lime-green variegated foliage*

### *Dracaena fragrans* 'Lemon Lime' ▷
### DRACAENA
↕ 3m (10ft) or more ↔ 1.2m (4ft) or more

One of the most colourful of a group famed for variegated foliage. The long, tapered leaves are lime green with a wide, cream-edged, dark green central stripe.

☼ Bright to moderate, avoiding summer sun 🌡 Warm. Moderate to high humidity 💧 Fortnightly. Occasionally in winter 💧 When dry. Water sparingly in winter 🌱 Tip cuttings, stem sections

### *Ficus bennendijkii* 'Alii' ▷
### FICUS
↕ 2m (6ft) or more
↔ 75cm (30in) or more

Looking like an evergreen weeping willow, this graceful houseplant has slender stems clothed in long, narrow leaves. Its fairly narrow habit makes it suitable for a variety of spaces.

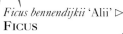

☼ Bright, but avoid summer sun 🌡 Warm. Moderate to high humidity 💧 Fortnightly. Occasionally in winter 💧 When compost surface dry. Reduce watering at lower temperatures 🌱 Tip cuttings, air layering

*Monstera deliciosa*
'Variegata' ▷
**SWISS CHEESE PLANT**
↕ ↔ 4m (12ft) or more

Grown on a moss pole,
this striking climber, with
outstanding, deeply-lobed,
green and white leaves, will
prove a talking point wherever
it is placed. If neglected or
allowed to dry out, it will
become an eyesore. ♔

☼ Bright to moderate ≣ Warm.
Moderate to high humidity
◖ Fortnightly. Occasionally in
winter ◊ Water when compost
surface just dry ▨ Stem cuttings, air layering

*Ravenea
rivularis* ▷
**MAJESTY
PALM**
↕ 3m (10ft) or more
↔ 1.5m (5ft) or more

A beautiful, quite fast-growing palm from Madagascar,
with elegant, feather-like leaves. A newcomer to indoor
cultivation, it tolerates low light and cool conditions.

☼ Bright to moderate, avoiding summer sun ≣ Moderate to warm.
Moderate to high humidity ◖ Fortnightly, using foliage houseplant
feed. Monthly in winter ◊ When dry. Avoid waterlogging ▨ Seed

*Murraya
paniculata* ▷
**ORANGE
JESSAMINE**
↕ 3m (10ft)
↔ 1.2m (4ft)

An attractive shrub with dark green,
divided, glossy, evergreen leaves, strongly
scented if bruised, and clusters of scented,
citrus-like flowers from spring to summer.

☼ Bright to moderate, with sun ≣ Moderate to
warm. Moderate to high humidity ◖ Fortnightly.
Occasionally in winter ◊ When compost surface
dry. Water sparingly in winter ▨ Semi-ripe cuttings

△ *Philodendron erubescens* 'Burgundy'
**BLUSHING PHILODENDRON**
↕ ↔ 3m (10ft) or more

Large, shining, red-flushed, red-veined
leaves are borne on dark purple-red
stems. Best trained on a moss pole, it is an
impressive plant when grown well. ♔

☼ Bright to shady ≣ Warm. Moderate to high
humidity ◖ Fortnightly, using foliage houseplant
fertilizer. Monthly in winter ◊ Let compost surface
dry slightly before watering ▨ Tip cuttings

△ *Spathiphyllum* 'Euro Gigant'
**PEACE LILY**
↕ ↔ 1m (3ft)

Magnificent at its best, and an excellent
specimen. Large, boldly-veined, paddle-
like green leaves are joined in spring and
summer by tall-stemmed white flowers.

☼ Bright, but avoid direct sun ≣ Moderate to
warm. Moderate to high humidity ◖ Fortnightly.
Monthly in winter ◊ Water when compost surface
dry. Avoid overwatering ▨ Division

LOCATIONS

73

# Houseplants for Sitting and Dining Rooms

IN MOST HOMES the sitting and dining rooms are the largest in the house. They are rooms to feel comfortable in, so all the more reason to include plants. Given their floor spaces, corners, and flat surfaces, they offer great potential for using plants to soften hard lines or edges, complement decor, and promote a relaxing atmosphere.

*Chlorophytum comosum* 'Variegatum' ▷
**SPIDER PLANT**
↕ 90cm (3ft) ↔ 60cm (2ft)

Easy and adaptable, this spider plant tolerates poor light and neglect, but thrives in good conditions. It differs from the equally common *Chlorophytum comosum* 'Vittatum' in having white, rather than green, leaf margins. ♔

☀ Bright to moderate, avoiding summer sun
≡ Moderate to warm. Moderate to high humidity
♦ Fortnightly. Stop at low winter temperatures
◊ Keep moist, but avoid waterlogging. In winter, water when compost surface dry ⌷ Plantlets

△ *Asparagus densiflorus* 'Myersii'
**FOXTAIL FERN**
↕ ↔ 45cm (18in)

This striking, tuberous-rooted foliage perennial has foxtail-like plumes of tiny, green, needle-like branchlets. Contrast with broad-leaved plants in a group. ♔

☀ Bright to moderate. Avoid hot sun ≡ Moderate to warm. Moderate humidity ♦ Foliage houseplant fertilizer weekly. Monthly in winter ◊ Keep moist. Water when dry in winter ⌷ Division

---

**OTHER FOLIAGE HOUSEPLANTS FOR SITTING AND DINING ROOMS**

*Aspidistra elatior* 'Milky Way', see p.66
*Dracaena fragrans* 'Massangeana',
   see p.77
*Monstera deliciosa*, see p.41
*Radermachera sinica*

---

*Asparagus falcatus* ▷
**SICKLETHORN**
↕ 3m (10ft) or more ↔ 1m (3ft)

An erect, strong-growing, bright green plant that in the wild clambers into trees by means of tiny spines. Grown indoors, it is more compact and easily controllable.

☀ Bright to moderate. Avoid hot sun ≡ Moderate to warm. Moderate humidity ♦ Foliage houseplant fertilizer weekly. Monthly in winter ◊ Keep moist. Water when dry in winter ⌷ Division, seed

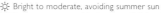

△ *Corynocarpus laevigatus*
**KARAKA**
↕ 3m (10ft) or more ↔ 1.5m (5ft) or more

In its native New Zealand the karaka is a woodland tree, but it is slower growing and easily controlled as a houseplant. It has handsome, shining, deep green leaves.

☀ Bright, with some direct sun ≡ Moderate to warm. Moderate humidity ♦ Monthly. Occasionally in winter ◊ When compost surface dry ⌷ Semi-ripe cuttings, seed

OTHER FLOWERING HOUSEPLANTS
FOR SITTING AND DINING ROOMS

*Heliotropium* 'Chatsworth'
*Impatiens walleriana* hybrids, see p.87
*Pelargonium* 'Sefton'
*Primula obconica*, see p.33
*Sinningia speciosa* cultivars

△ *Dracaena cincta* 'Tricolor'
## DRACAENA
↕ 3m (10ft) ↔ 1.2m (4ft)

A slow-growing shrub or small tree with
slender stems and loose ruffs of long,
narrow, shining green leaves, striped
cream and stained pink along the margins.

☼ Bright to moderate, avoiding direct summer sun
≣ Warm. Moderate to high humidity
◗ Fortnightly. Occasionally in winter ◊ When
compost surface dry. Water sparingly
in winter 🌱 Tip or stem cuttings

△ *Justicia carnea*
## FLAMINGO PLANT
↕ 1.2m (4ft) ↔ 80cm (32in)

This evergreen shrub produces large,
boldly-veined leaves and dense spikes of
two-lipped, pink to rose-pink flowers in
summer or later. Keep bushy by pruning.

☼ Bright to moderate, avoiding direct sun
≣ Warm, avoiding draughts. Moderate to high
humidity ◗ Monthly ◊ Keep moist, but avoid
waterlogging 🌱 Semi-ripe cuttings, seed

*Peperomia
caperata*
'Lilian' ▷
## PEPEROMIA
↕ 20cm (8in) ↔ 15cm (6in)

The neat tuft of corrugated, deep green
leaves is topped by white flower spikes in
late summer. An ideal plant for growing in
a small space, bottle garden, or terrarium.

☼ Bright to moderate, with some sun ≣ Warm.
Moderate to high humidity ◗ Every three weeks.
Occasionally in winter ◊ When compost surface
dry. Avoid waterlogging 🌱 Tip cuttings

*Hibiscus rosa-
sinensis* 'Lateritia' ▷
## ROSE OF CHINA
↕ 2.5m (8ft) ↔ 1.5m (5ft)

Roses of China are capable of
reaching a large size but can be
pruned in winter to encourage a
more bushy, compact habit. Large,
yellow, deep-throated flowers
appear from spring to autumn.

☼ Bright ≣ Warm, avoiding fluctuation.
Moderate to high humidity ◗ Fortnightly. Stop
feeding at lower temperatures ◊ When
compost surface just dry. Water sparingly in
winter 🌱 Tip cuttings

△ *Pericallis* x *hybrida* cultivars
## FLORISTS' CINERARIA
↕ 30cm (12in) ↔ 25cm (10in)

Spectacular winter- to spring-flowering
plants, these have a rosette of bold foliage
crowned by usually long-lasting, large,
daisy-like flowers in a variety of colours.

☼ Bright, but avoid direct sun ≣ Cool to
moderate or warm. Moderate to high humidity
◗ Fortnightly ◊ Keep moist, but avoid waterlogging
🌱 Seed

LOCATIONS

# Houseplants for Bedrooms

**I**T WAS ONCE commonly believed that plants in a bedroom or hospital ward, certainly at night, were injurious to health. This misconception may have stemmed from the fact that the leaves of most plants absorb oxygen during the hours of darkness. Nowadays we know that plants in an airy bedroom will provide benefits including increased humidity, a reduction in chemical toxins, and the suppression of airborne microbes. Carefully placed, the house-plants shown here can bring a healthy, relaxing atmosphere to any bedroom.

LOCATIONS

*Achimenes* hybrids ▷
### HOT WATER PLANT
↕ ↔ 30cm (12in)

Blooming profusely from summer into autumn, few houseplants are more free-flowering. Support the floppy stems or grow in a hanging basket or on a pedestal.

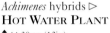

☼ Bright. Avoid summer sun ▮ Warm. Moderate humidity ♦ Fortnightly, using flowering houseplant fertilizer ◊ Freely in summer; reduce in autumn; keep dry in winter; increase in spring ▨ Tubercles

*Asparagus umbellatus* ▷
### ASPARAGUS FERN
↕ 1.2m (4ft) ↔ 60cm (2ft)

The asparagus fern makes a cheerful informal houseplant with its clusters of bristle-like, bright green leaves. In its native Canary Islands it is a scrambling perennial, so if pot-grown the stems may need support.

☼ Bright to moderate, avoiding summer sun ▮ Moderate to warm. Moderate humidity ♦ Foliage houseplant fertilizer weekly. Monthly in winter ◊ Keep moist. In winter, water when dry ▨ Division, seed

*Aglaonema* 'Lilian' ▷
### CHINESE EVERGREEN
↕ ↔ 60cm (2ft)

This Chinese evergreen produces small, arum-like flowers in summer, but is valued most for its beautifully marked, slender-pointed leaves, borne in a bold clump. Slow-growing but well worth it.

☼ Moderate, avoiding sun ▮ Moderate to warm. Moderate to high humidity ♦ Foliage houseplant fertilizer weekly. Monthly in winter ◊ When dry ▨ Division, tip cuttings

*Catharanthus roseus* ▷
### MADAGASCAR PERIWINKLE
↕ ↔ 30cm (12in)

This easy-to-grow plant forms a low, rounded bush of shiny foliage, and sports large pink, lavender, white, red, or periwinkle flowers from late spring to autumn. ⚱

☼ Bright, but avoid summer sun ▮ Warm. Moderate humidity ♦ Monthly ◊ Water regularly, keeping permanently moist. Avoid waterlogging ▨ Tip cuttings. Roots easily in water

*Pilea microphylla* ▷
**ARTILLERY PLANT**
↕ ↔ 30cm (12in)

This compact pilea forms a small hummock of foliage. It derives its common name from the pollen, which silently and harmlessly "explodes" when ripe. Suitable for a sunless position and best regarded as a temporary plant.

☼ Moderate ⧉ Moderate to warm. Moderate to high humidity ♦ Fortnightly. Monthly in winter ♦ Water when compost surface just dry. Avoid waterlogging ⧉ Tip cuttings

### OTHER FOLIAGE HOUSEPLANTS FOR BEDROOMS

*Adiantum raddianum*, see p.100
*Aspidistra elatior*, see p.88
*Chlorophytum comosum* 'Vittatum', see p.86
*Dracaena fragrans* 'White Edge'
*Nephrolepis exaltata* 'Bostoniensis', see p.109

△ *Solenostemon* 'Wizard'
**COLEUS, FLAME NETTLE**
↕ ↔ 20cm (8in)

Brilliantly coloured leaves are the trademark of coleus; this wide-margined form is excellent for a sunny window or well-lit spot. Pinch out tips for compact growth.

☼ Bright ⧉ Warm. Moderate humidity ♦ Weekly. Occasionally in winter ♦ Keep moist, but avoid waterlogging. In winter, water when just dry ⧉ Tip cuttings, seed. Roots easily in water

△ *Dracaena fragrans* 'Massangeana'
**CORN PALM**
↕ 3m (10ft) ↔ 1.2m (4ft)

The stout stems form a miniature tree crowded with glossy green leaves with a greenish-yellow central band. One of the most popular of all dracaenas. ♔

☼ Bright to moderate, avoiding summer sun ⧉ Warm. Moderate to high humidity ♦ Fortnightly. Occasionally in winter ♦ When compost surface dry. Water sparingly in winter ⧉ Tip cuttings, stem sections

### OTHER FLOWERING HOUSEPLANTS FOR BEDROOMS

*Begonia tuberosa* hybrids
*Cyclamen persicum* hybrids, see p.32
*Impatiens walleriana* hybrids, see p.87
*Oxalis purpurata*, see p.49
*Spathiphyllum* 'Euro Gigant', see p.73

*Dracaena reflexa* 'Song of India' ▷
**DRACAENA**
↕ 3m (10ft) ↔ 1.2m (4ft)

Many-branched and woody-stemmed, this plant eventually grows into a small tree. Its yellow-margined leaves are mostly crowded towards the branch ends.

☼ Bright to moderate, avoiding summer sun ⧉ Warm. Moderate to high humidity ♦ Fortnightly. Occasionally in winter ♦ When dry. Water sparingly in winter ⧉ Tip cuttings, stem sections

△ *Syngonium podophyllum* 'Pixie'
**GOOSEFOOT PLANT**
↕ ↔ 30cm (12in)

White-marbled, arrow-shaped leaves, initially clump-forming, divide as this attractive perennial matures and begins to climb. Best grown on a moss pole.

☼ Bright to moderate, avoiding summer sun ⧉ Warm, avoiding fluctuation. Moderate to high humidity ♦ Fortnightly. Monthly in winter ♦ When compost surface dry ⧉ Tip cuttings

**LOCATIONS**

# Houseplants for Narrow Spaces

EVERY HOME contains awkward narrow spaces, perhaps with restricted access, which call for small or upright plants rather than large or bushy specimens. They are just the spots to take most climbers, trailers, or compact, well-mannered plants that respond well to occasional pruning. Such situations can be poorly lit, so choose plants that will tolerate a degree of shade.

*Handsome, glossy leaves*

## *Asparagus setaceus* 'Nanus' ▷
### ASPARAGUS FERN
↕ ↔ 45cm (18in)

The delicate, feathery, frond-like foliage of this plant is commonly used in button-holes. Unlike the parent species, this compact form will not climb and is ideal for small spaces.

☼ Bright to moderate, avoiding summer sun ❄ Cool to warm. Moderate humidity
💧 Weekly, using foliage houseplant fertilizer. Monthly in winter ○ Keep moist. When compost surface dry at lower temperatures ✉ Division, seed

> OTHER SMALL HOUSE-
> PLANTS FOR NARROW SPACES
>
> *Achimenes* hybrids
> *Ardisia crispa*
> *Cyperus involucratus* 'Nanus'
> *Ficus pumila* 'White Sonny', see p.65
> *Spathiphyllum* 'Petite'

## *Cissus antarctica* ▷
### KANGAROO VINE
↕ 3m (10ft) ↔ 60cm (2ft)

This vigorous Australian plant produces attractive, glossy, dark green, leathery leaves with scalloped edges. Provide support, and pinch out the growing tips to control its height and spread. 🏆

☼ Bright to moderate, avoiding summer sun
❄ Cool to warm. Moderate to high humidity
💧 Fortnightly. Monthly in winter, at higher temperatures ○ When compost surface dry. Avoid underwatering ✉ Tip cuttings

## △ *Cissus rhombifolia* 'Ellen Danica'
### GRAPE IVY
↕ 2m (6ft) ↔ 45cm (18in)

As it climbs by tendrils, train this popular form of grape ivy on a trellis or canes to display its large, glossy, deeply lobed leaves. Young plants are best grown as trailers. Full of character. 🏆

☼ Bright to moderate, avoiding summer sun
❄ Cool to warm. Moderate to high humidity
💧 Fortnightly. Monthly in winter, at higher temperatures ○ Allow to dry out before watering. Avoid underwatering ✉ Tip cuttings

△ *Crocus vernus* cultivars
**DUTCH CROCUS**
↕ 12cm (5in) ↔ 5cm (2in)

Giving a cheerful late winter or spring display in a cool part of the house, this old favourite, with goblet-shaped flowers in many colours, brightens any narrow space.

☼ Bright ◧ Cool to moderate. Moderate humidity ◊ Unnecessary ◊ Keep moist, but avoid waterlogging ⬚ Cormlets. In temperate climates, crocuses can be planted outdoors after flowering

---

**OTHER TALL HOUSEPLANTS OR CLIMBERS FOR NARROW SPACES**

*Dieffenbachia* 'Compacta', see p.40
*Dracaena fragrans* 'Compacta', see p.64
*Ficus bennendijkii* 'Alii', see p.72
*Hedera helix* 'Ivalace'
*Schefflera arboricola* 'Compacta', see p.91
*Yucca elephantipes*, see p.87

---

△ × *Fatshedera lizei* 'Pia'
**FATSHEDERA**
↕ 2m (6ft) ↔ 45cm (18in)

An excellent foliage shrub with glossy, five-lobed, wavy-edged leaves. Grow several together against a pale background to emphasize their leaf shape and form.

☼ Moderate. Tolerates some shade ◧ Cool to warm. Moderate humidity ◊ Foliage houseplant fertilizer fortnightly. Monthly in winter ◊ Water when dry ⬚ Tip cuttings, stem sections

---

△ *Hedera helix* 'Ovata'
**COMMON IVY, ENGLISH IVY**
↕ 2m (6ft) ↔ 30cm (12in)

This ivy has leathery, unlobed, deep green, triangular leaves, sometimes with wedge-shaped tips. Grow it in a hanging basket or train it up a pole or frame. Sometimes sold as 'Mein Hertz'.

☼ Bright to moderate ◧ Cool to warm. Moderate to high humidity ◊ Fortnightly. Twice in winter ◊ When compost surface dry. Water sparingly in winter ⬚ Tip cuttings, layering

---

△ *Euonymus japonicus* 'Aureus'
**JAPANESE SPINDLE**
↕ 1.5m (5ft) ↔ 60cm (2ft)

Ideal for a cool room or hallway, this delightful, slow-growing, compact plant has gold-splashed, dark green leaves. Can be planted outside if it grows too large.

☼ Bright, with some direct sun ◧ Cool to warm. Moderate humidity ◊ Monthly, from spring to autumn ◊ When compost surface dry. Water sparingly in winter ⬚ Tip cuttings

---

△ *Hedera canariensis* 'Montgomery'
**CANARY ISLAND IVY**
↕ 4m (12ft) ↔ 1m (3ft)

Decorative bronze-purple stems produce large, sharply lobed, mid-green leaves that become a dark glossy green with maturity. May need restrictive pruning with age.

☼ Bright to moderate ◧ Cool to warm. Moderate to high humidity ◊ Fortnightly. Twice in winter ◊ When compost surface dry. Water sparingly in winter ⬚ Tip cuttings, layering

---

△ *Tolmiea menziesii* 'Taff's Gold'
**PIGGYBACK PLANT**
↕ ↔ 30cm (12in)

Small plantlets occur where each leaf and stalk join, hence the common name of this plant with hairy, gold-mottled green leaves. A good choice for a cool spot.

☼ Bright, but avoid direct sun ◧ Cool to moderate. Moderate humidity ◊ Fortnightly. Twice in winter, if temperature raised ◊ When compost surface dry. Water sparingly in winter ⬚ Plantlets

# Houseplants for Garden Rooms

△ *Euryops chrysanthemoides*
**EURYOPS**
↕ 1m (3ft) ↔ 1.2m (4ft) or more

GARDEN ROOMS, offering protection from unfavourable weather yet benefiting from unrestricted light, are often the ideal way to provide houseplants with optimum growing conditions, particularly in cool temperate climates. Artificial, consistent heat and humidity levels allow tropical species to grow, but a wide range of plants will thrive even in a cool garden room.

*Anigozanthos flavidus* ▷
**KANGAROO PAW**
↕ 1.2m (4ft) ↔ 45cm (18in)

Curiously shaped flowers, in either pink or yellow, are produced in clusters in late spring or summer and give this plant its common name. A near-hardy plant that is suitable for a cooler garden room.

☀ Bright to moderate, avoiding summer sun
🌡 Moderate to warm. Moderate humidity 💧 Fortnightly, using fertilizer for ericaceous plants. Occasionally in winter 💧 Keep moist. Reduce watering in winter 🏵 Division, seed

Worth growing for the cheerful, bright yellow daisy flowers alone. These are borne intermittently throughout the year over a dense, dome-shaped bush of rich green foliage. It can be pruned to maintain the required shape.

☀ Bright, with sun 🌡 Moderate to warm. Moderate humidity 💧 Every three weeks 💧 When compost surface dry. Water sparingly in winter 🏵 Semi-ripe cuttings, seed

---

**OTHER HOUSEPLANTS FOR GARDEN ROOMS**

*Coronilla valentina* subsp. *glauca*
*Eupatorium sordidum*
*Leonotis ocymifolia*
*Lithodora rosmarinifolia*
*Metrosideros kermadecensis* 'Variegatus'
*Prostanthera rotundifolia*, see p.47

---

△ *Argyranthemum* 'Vancouver'
**CANARY ISLAND MARGUERITE**
↕ ↔ 90cm (3ft)

Abundant, anemone-centred pink flowers, from spring to autumn, give this perennial a long season of interest. Deadheading regularly will encourage more blooms. 🏆

☀ Bright, but avoid direct sun 🌡 Cool to moderate. Moderate humidity 💧 Every three weeks 💧 Keep moist, but avoid waterlogging 🏵 Tip cuttings

*Tiny flowers with spreading petals*

*Cuphea hyssopifolia* ▷
**FALSE HEATHER**
↕ 60cm (2ft) ↔ 80cm (32in)

Bushy and compact, narrow-leaved false heathers are sometimes used as summer bedding plants in cool climates. Masses of small pink, purple, or white flowers are freely produced from summer through to autumn. 🏆

☀ Bright, avoiding direct sun 🌡 Cool to moderate. Moderate humidity 💧 Every three weeks. Occasionally in winter 💧 When compost surface dry. Water sparingly in winter 🏵 Tip cuttings

△ *Pelargonium* 'Carisbrooke'
## REGAL PELARGONIUM
↕ 45cm (18in) ↔ 30cm (12in)

Broad clusters of pale rose-pink flowers, their upper petals blazed with claret, are produced in a flowering season of short duration, from spring to midsummer. ▽

☼ Bright, with sun ▤ Moderate to warm, but cool in winter. Moderate humidity ◑ Fortnightly, using high potash fertilizer ◌ When compost surface just dry. Water sparingly in winter ▥ Tip cuttings

△ *Rehmannia elata*
## CHINESE FOXGLOVE
↕ 75cm (30in) or more ↔ 45cm (18in)

Loose-stemmed and downy all over, this perennial member of the foxglove family produces gorgeous, pendulous, pinkish-purple flowers from summer into autumn.

☼ Bright ▤ Moderate to warm. Moderate humidity ◑ Monthly. Occasionally in winter ◌ When compost surface dry. Water sparingly in winter ▥ Seed

*Spectacular creamy-pink flowers*

△ *Pittosporum tobira*
## JAPANESE MOCK ORANGE
↕ ↔ 2m (6ft) or more

Creamy flower clusters, appearing in late spring and summer, are deliciously scented of orange-blossom. Attractive, glossy evergreen foliage sets off the flowers and can be pruned into shape. ▽

☼ Bright, with some sun ▤ Moderate to warm, but cool in winter. Moderate humidity ◑ Fortnightly. Occasionally in winter ◌ When dry. Water sparingly in winter ▥ Semi-ripe cuttings, seed

### OTHER CLIMBING HOUSEPLANTS FOR GARDEN ROOMS

*Bomarea caldasii*
*Jasminum polyanthum*, see p.25
*Passiflora* 'Amethyst', see p.94
*Plumbago auriculata*
*Streptosolen jamesonii*

△ *Strelitzia reginae*
## BIRD OF PARADISE
↕ 1.5m (5ft) ↔ 1m (3ft)

Instantly recognizable when in flower, this spectacular South African exotic also has a bold clump of handsome paddle-shaped leaves. Plants take several years to flower; the distinctive blooms last several weeks. ▽

☼ Bright, with sun ▤ Moderate to warm. Moderate humidity ◑ Fortnightly. Occasionally in winter ◌ When compost surface dry. Water sparingly in winter ▥ Division, seed

◁ *Zantedeschia* 'Little Suzie'
## ARUM LILY
↕ ↔ 60cm (2ft)

Given sufficient moisture during the growing season, this plant will produce a lush clump of foliage, through which the creamy-pink flowers emerge in summer. It is dormant in winter.

☼ Bright, but avoid intense summer sun ▤ Moderate to warm. Moderate humidity ◑ Fortnightly ◌ Keep moist. Reduce watering during resting period ▥ Division, offsets

# Houseplants for the Home Office

NOWADAYS MANY PEOPLE work from home. Growing plants in a home office (or any workplace) will improve air quality, adding moisture and helping to disperse pollutants including computer emissions; they may even help you think more clearly. Stand plants away from your equipment to prevent watering accidents.

△ *Crassula ovata*
**JADE PLANT**
‡ ↔ 1m (3ft) or more

One of the easiest houseplants, this slowly forms a small- to medium-sized succulent bush with red-tinted green foliage. White or pink flowers appear in autumn. ♆

☼ Bright, sunny ◗▮ Warm, but moderate in winter. Low humidity ◖ Monthly, using fertilizer for cacti and succulents ◊ When compost surface dry. Water sparingly in winter ▨ Tip or leaf cuttings

---

**OTHER FLOWERING HOUSE-PLANTS FOR THE HOME OFFICE**

*Anthurium* 'Lady Jane'
*Gerbera jamesonii*
*Impatiens walleriana* hybrids, see p.87
*Kalanchoe blossfeldiana*
*Pelargonium* 'Stellar Apricot'
*Schlumbergera* x *buckleyi*
*Schlumbergera truncata*, see p.65

---

△ *Aglaonema* 'Maria Christina'
**CHINESE EVERGREEN**
‡ ↔ 50cm (20in)

A suckering, clump-forming perennial producing handsome, large, upright green leaves, liberally splashed and striped creamy white and pale green.

☼ Moderate, avoiding summer sun ◗▮ Moderate to warm. Moderate to high humidity ◖ Weekly, using foliage houseplant fertilizer. Monthly in winter ◊ When dry ▨ Division, tip or stem cuttings

△ *Adiantum raddianum* 'Fritz Luth'
**MAIDENHAIR FERN**
‡ ↔ 60cm (2ft)

One of the best maidenhair ferns when mature, with beautifully segmented, emerald-green fronds on wiry, shining black stalks. Protect from cold draughts.

☼ Moderate, avoiding direct sun ◗▮ Moderate to warm. Moderate to high humidity ◖ Fortnightly. Monthly in winter ◊ Keep moist, but avoid waterlogging ▨ Division, spores

*Aechmea fasciata* 'Morgana' ▷
**URN PLANT**
‡ 60cm (2ft) ↔ 75cm (30in)

The big, funnel-shaped rosette of lilac-grey leaves is enhanced in summer by a spectacular, rose-pink, bracted flower-head. A splendid exotic for a pot or hanging basket in the right spot.

☼ Bright, but avoid summer sun ◗▮ Warm. Moderate to high humidity ◖ Fortnightly ◊ When compost surface dry. Water sparingly in winter. Keep "urn" topped up with water ▨ Offsets

△ *Cryptanthus bivittatus*
**EARTH STAR**
‡ 10cm (4in) ↔ 25cm (10in)

A curious-looking plant bearing flattened, star-shaped rosettes of sharply-pointed, wavy-margined, green and white-striped leaves; the white may turn pink in sun. ♆

☼ Bright to shady, avoiding direct sun ◗▮ Warm. High humidity. Mist regularly or stand on pebble tray ◖ Monthly, using flowering houseplant fertilizer. Twice during winter ◊ When top 5cm (2in) of compost dries out ▨ Offsets

*Pale green and yellow variegation*

*Ctenanthe* 'Golden Mosaic' ▷
**CTENANTHE**
↕ ↔ 1m (3ft)

This handsome foliage plant from Brazil forms clumps of cane-like stems that bear deep green leaves, marked with paler green and creamy-yellow streaks and patches. Grow ctenanthes in a pebble tray for best results.

☼ Bright to moderate, avoiding direct sun ◰ Warm, avoiding fluctuation. High humidity ◔ Fortnightly, using foliage houseplant fertilizer. Rarely in winter ◌ Keep compost moist. In cool winter temperatures, water when dry ⛏ Division

---

**OTHER FOLIAGE HOUSEPLANTS FOR THE HOME OFFICE**

*Cissus rhombifolia* 'Ellen Danica', see p.78
*Dracaena marginata*, see p.97
*Ficus benjamina*, see p.86
*Hedera helix* 'Ivalace'
*Nephrolepis exaltata* 'Bostoniensis', see p.109
*Pelargonium* 'Graveolens', see p.46
*Philodendron tuxtlanum* 'Tuxtla'
*Sansevieria trifasciata*, see p.89
*Yucca elephantipes*, see p.87

---

△ *Pilea peperomioides*
**PILEA**
↕ ↔ 30cm (12in)

This easy-to-grow plant from south-west China tolerates neglect, but treat it well to make the most of its glossy, dark green, shield-like, long-stalked, succulent leaves.

☼ Bright to moderate, with some sun ◰ Warm. Moderate to high humidity ◔ Every three weeks. Occasionally in winter ◌ When compost surface just dry. Avoid waterlogging ⛏ Tip cuttings

◁ *Dieffenbachia seguine* 'Tropic Snow'
**DUMB CANE**
↕ ↔ 1m (3ft)

Grow this plant for its bold green foliage marked with pale green and cream variegation; the large leaves give out plenty of water, counteracting dry air. Thrives best on a pebble tray. It is poisonous if chewed, so keep out of the reach of small children.

☼ Bright to moderate. Avoid hot sun ◰ Moderate to warm. Moderate to high humidity ◔ Fortnightly, using foliage houseplant fertilizer. Monthly in winter ◌ When dry ⛏ Tip or stem cuttings

△ *Spathiphyllum wallisii* 'Clevelandii'
**PEACE LILY**
↕ 65cm (26in) ↔ 50cm (20in)

Peace lilies filter toxins from the air and can tolerate low light, so they are useful for an office corner. Display their showy foliage and white flowers to advantage.

☼ Bright to moderate, avoiding direct sun ◰ Moderate to warm. Moderate to high humidity ◔ Fortnightly. Monthly in winter ◌ When compost surface dry. Avoid overwatering ⛏ Division

**LOCATIONS**

# SPECIFIC USES

HOUSEPLANTS ARE without doubt one of the most versatile of all plant groups, with a huge choice for every specific decorative or cultural requirement. Whether you need an architectural form, a selection for a terrarium, or an easy-to-grow houseplant, in the following pages you will find a plant that fits the bill.

△ WINTER ORNAMENT *This collection of solanums and capsicums makes the most of the brightly coloured, decorative fruits, and provides winter colour.*

*Homalomena wallisii to improve air quality*

There are still many people who are convinced that all houseplants are difficult to grow. Beginners can take heart and try some of the many houseplants that are easy and totally reliable. Some will even tolerate neglect and survive in adverse conditions, although this should never be a reason to forget them. Some flowering plants are hardy and can be planted outside after blooming, giving you two uses

for the price of one. All plants produce oxygen as well as absorb impurities from the air, so growing plants indoors is one of the easiest ways of maintaining a healthy home environment.

### APPEALING HABITS
The growth habit of some plants, such as climbers and slender-stemmed or trailing plants, is their most interesting and useful feature. Grow trailers in hanging baskets designed for indoor use or in pots placed on raised surfaces such as shelves and cupboards. Such plants can even be used to create a living "curtain" of growth. Equally, many climbers can be trained on to moss poles or frames, providing interest for narrow spaces and awkward

corners. Architectural plants that offer impressive forms make fine specimen plants if you have room.

### OTHER USES
Many plants from tropical rain-forests demand heat and humidity in order to thrive. Such plants, especially slow-growing or dwarf varieties, can be housed in glazed terraria, glass-panelled tanks, or bell jars, which can become very impressive features. Ornamental fruits or seedheads, like the bright cherry-sized fruits of solanums, are particularly eye-catching in the home, often providing much-needed winter interest. Or why not grow culinary herbs in pots on a sunny kitchen windowsill – a fresh supply is a bonus to any cook.

△ EASY TO GROW *This* Aloe variegata *can withstand neglect, and so can be used where it may be temporarily forgotten.*

◁ HERBS FOR THE KITCHEN *Herbs for cooking can be grown on any warm windowsill or ledge; in the kitchen, they will be close to hand for harvesting.*

▷ ARCHITECTURAL VALUE *Elephant's foot plants, with their curved trunk and curious top-knot of leaves, look most striking when displayed as specimens.*

# Houseplants for Beginners

NOTHING ENCOURAGES more than success, which breeds both confidence and the desire to know more. This is certainly true of growing houseplants, and there is a wide range of reliable plants that are particularly suitable for first-time growers. They include plants with a variety of leaf and flower forms, and habits from small to architectural. Most are relatively easy to propagate; when you succeed in caring for these plants, then grow some for your friends.

*Echeveria secunda* var. *glauca* 'Gigantea' ▷
**ECHEVERIA**
↕ 8cm (3in) ↔ 15cm (6in)

Grow this striking succulent for its large rosettes of blue-grey fleshy leaves with red-bristled tips. Clusters of red and yellow flowers appear in early summer.

☼ Bright ☷ Warm, but cool in winter. Low humidity ◊ Every three weeks, using cactus or high potash fertilizer ◊ When top 2.5cm (1in) dry. Water sparingly in winter, if shrivelling ▭ Leaf cuttings, offsets

△ *Chlorophytum comosum* 'Vittatum'
**SPIDER PLANT**
↕ 90cm (3ft) ↔ 60cm (2ft)

One of the most popular houseplants, with boldly striped leaves and pale, arching stems bearing white starry summer flowers that are replaced by little plantlets. Good in a hanging basket. ▽

☼ Bright to moderate, avoiding summer sun ☷ Moderate to warm. Moderate to high humidity ◊ Fortnightly. Stop feeding at low winter temperatures ◊ Keep moist, but avoid water-logging. Water when dry at low winter temperatures ▭ Plantlets

*Pendent branches with small leaves*

*Cyperus involucratus* 'Gracilis' ▷
**UMBRELLA PLANT**
↕ 45cm (18in) ↔ 30cm (12in) or more

A curious, clump-forming sedge with narrow, leafy green bracts crowded at the ends of the erect shoots. The umbrella plant provides a good contrast to ferns or broad-leaved plants.

*Ficus benjamina* ▷
**WEEPING FIG**
↕ 2.2m (7ft) ↔ 75cm (30in)

This is an excellent houseplant, well worth growing for its tree-like habit, weeping branches, and small, neatly-pointed leaves. It will occupy plenty of space when mature. ▽

☼ Bright to shady, avoiding direct sun ☷ Warm. Moderate to high humidity ◊ Fortnightly, using foliage houseplant fertilizer. Occasionally in winter ◊ Likes to be waterlogged. It is impossible to overwater this plant ▭ Division

☼ Bright, but avoid summer sun ☷ Moderate to warm, avoiding fluctuation. Moderate to high humidity ◊ Fortnightly. Occasionally in winter ◊ When compost surface dry. Reduce watering at lower temperatures ▭ Tip cuttings

OTHER SUCCULENT
HOUSEPLANTS FOR BEGINNERS

*Faucaria tigrina*, see p.57
*Kalanchoe pumila*, see p.31
*Oscularia caulescens*
*Pachyphytum oviferum*, see p.111
*Portulaca socialis*
*Sedum morganianum*, see p.111

△ *Impatiens walleriana* hybrids
**BUSY LIZZIE**
↕ 30cm (12in) ↔ 35cm (14in)

This very well-known flowering plant has fleshy stems and colourful, slender-spurred blooms throughout summer. The hybrids come in a dazzling array of shades.

☀ Bright ≣ Warm. Moderate to high humidity ▲ Fortnightly. Occasionally in winter ○ When compost surface dry ✂ Tip cuttings, seed. Roots easily in water

△ *Saxifraga* 'Tricolor'
**MOTHER OF THOUSANDS**
↕ ↔ 30cm (12in)

Display this plant in a hanging basket or pot on a raised surface where its slender red runners, ending in little plantlets, can hang free. The richly variegated leaves are eye-catching. 🏆

☀ Bright, with some direct sun ≣ Cool to moderate, but cooler in winter. Moderate humidity ▲ Fortnightly ○ When dry. Sparingly in cool conditions ✂ Division, plantlets

△ *Tradescantia zebrina*
**INCH PLANT, WANDERING JEW**
↕ ↔ 45cm (18in) or more

Fast-growing and fleshy-stemmed, this popular perennial is a splendid trailing plant for a hanging basket. The leaf surfaces are fascinating in detail. 🏆

☀ Bright to moderate ≣ Warm. Moderate to high humidity ▲ Fortnightly. Rarely in winter ○ Water when compost surface dry ✂ Division, tip cuttings

△ *Sansevieria trifasciata* 'Laurentii'
**MOTHER-IN-LAW'S TONGUE**
↕ 1.2m (4ft) ↔ 75cm (30in)

Shown here is the most popular form of this well-known plant. The upright, thick, succulent, dark green, gold-edged leaves are borne from an underground stem. 🏆

☀ Bright to moderate ≣ Moderate to warm. Low humidity ▲ Fortnightly ○ When compost surface dry. Water sparingly in winter. Avoid overwatering ✂ Division

OTHER HOUSEPLANTS FOR
BEGINNERS

*Asparagus setaceus*
*Aspidistra elatior*, see p.88
*Euphorbia milii* var. *tulearensis*, see p.88
*Haworthia attenuata*, see p.89
*Hedera helix* 'Eva', see p.53
*Plectranthus australis*
*Schlumbergera truncata*, see p.65
*Tolmiea menziesii* 'Taff's Gold', see p.79

△ *Yucca elephantipes*
**SPINELESS YUCCA**
↕ 2.5m (8ft) ↔ 2m (6ft)

Presented for sale with its sawn-off stems, this plant looks like an oddity. But it soon grows into a bold exotic specimen, with long, sword-shaped, leathery leaves. 🏆

☀ Bright, with some direct sun ≣ Moderate to warm, but cooler in winter. Low humidity ▲ Fortnightly ○ Keep moist. Water sparingly at lower temperatures ✂ Stem cuttings

SPECIFIC USES

# Houseplants Tolerant of Neglect

$\mathcal{S}$OME PLANTS can survive the toughest conditions – high, low, or fluctuating temperatures and light levels, waterlogging, drought, or starvation. This resilience makes them perfect for students, workaholics, or non-gardeners who want living colour and interest at home. These plants all tolerate neglect, but with care, they'll flourish.

SPECIFIC USES

*Aloe variegata* ▷
## PARTRIDGE-BREASTED ALOE
↕ 26cm (10in) ↔ 17cm (7in)

This compact succulent has overlapping, triangular, white-marked leaves. Salmon-pink flowers are borne from late winter to early spring, after a winter rest. ♔

☼ Bright to moderate ❄ Warm. Moderate to cool winter rest. Low humidity ◐ Every three weeks, using fertilizer for cacti and succulents ◌ When top 5cm (2in) dry. Sparingly in winter ⌹ Offsets

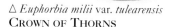

△ *Euphorbia milii* var. *tulearensis*
## CROWN OF THORNS
↕ ↔ 1m (3ft)

One of the toughest of all houseplants, and one of the spiniest too, so position it with care. Clusters of showy, pink-bracted flowers appear in spring or summer. ♔

☼ Bright, with sun ❄ Moderate to warm. Low humidity ◐ Every three weeks, using fertilizer for cacti and succulents ◌ When dry. Reduce in winter. Overwatering causes leaf loss ⌹ Stem cuttings

△ *Asparagus densiflorus* 'Sprengeri'
## EMERALD FERN
↕ ↔ 80cm (32in)

The fine, ferny "leaves" of this South African plant are actually flattened stems. A graceful habit and cheerful bright green foliage make this an invaluable plant. ♔

☼ Bright to moderate, avoiding sun ❄ Moderate to warm. Moderate humidity ◐ Weekly, using foliage houseplant fertilizer. Monthly in winter ◌ Keep moist. Reduce in winter ⌹ Division

△ *Aspidistra elatior*
## CAST IRON PLANT
↕ ↔ 60cm (2ft)

A "must" for every home, this almost indestructible Victorian favourite tolerates low light, draughts, and fluctuating temperatures, as its name suggests. ♔

☼ Moderate to shady. Direct sun scorches leaves ❄ Moderate to warm. Moderate to high humidity ◐ Every three weeks ◌ Water when compost surface dry. Dislikes waterlogging ⌹ Division

△ *Ferocactus latispinus*
## FISH-HOOK CACTUS
↕ 25cm (10in) ↔ 38cm (15in)

Spiny and ferocious-looking, this cactus from the Mexican desert can survive heat, cold, and long periods of drought. With care, it may bear violet flowers in summer.

☼ Bright ❄ Warm, but moderate to cool winter rest. Low humidity ◐ Every three weeks, using fertilizer for cacti and succulents ◌ When top 5cm (2in) dry. Sparingly in winter if shrivelling ⌹ Offsets

△ *Haworthia attenuata*
### ZEBRA HAWORTHIA
↕ ↔ 13cm (5in)

Neat and compact, this succulent has leaves covered with white pustules, and bears long-lasting, creamy-white flowers in summer. Ideal for a narrow windowsill.

☀ Bright ☷ Warm, with moderate to cool winter rest. Low humidity ♦ Every three weeks, using fertilizer for cacti and succulents ◊ When top 5cm (2in) compost dry. Sparingly in winter ⌸ Offsets

### OTHER HOUSEPLANTS TOLERANT OF NEGLECT

*Aloe vera*
*Asparagus setaceus*
*Chlorophytum comosum* 'Vittatum', see p.86
*Cissus antarctica*, see p.78
*Crassula arborescens*, see p.62
*Crassula ovata*, see p.82
*Echeveria* 'Black Prince'
*Euphorbia obesa*, see p.69
*Kalanchoe daigremontiana*
*Kalanchoe pumila*, see p.31
*Kalanchoe tomentosa*, see p.45
*Orbea variegata*, see p.110
*Pachypodium lamerei*, see p.111
*Plectranthus australis*
*Tolmiea menziesii*, see p.67

*Sansevieria trifasciata* ▷
### SNAKE PLANT
↕ 1.2m (4ft) ↔ 75cm (30in)

Grow the snake plant for its elegant, variegated, sword-shaped leaves. Underground rhizomes store water for times of drought. This plant will survive anything but waterlogging or constant repotting; only repot if it is too congested.

☀ Bright to moderate ☷ Moderate to warm. Low humidity ♦ Monthly ◊ When compost surface dry. Water sparingly in winter. Avoid overwatering ⌸ Division, leaf cuttings or sections

*Sparrmannia africana* ▷
### HOUSE LIME
↕ ↔ 2m (6ft) or more

A large, vigorous South African shrub with bold, downy foliage and, in late summer, clusters of white, yellow-stamened flowers. Prune after flowering to encourage more blooms.

☀ Bright, but avoid direct sun ☷ Moderate to warm. Moderate humidity ♦ Fortnightly, using high potash fertilizer ◊ When compost surface dry. Reduce in winter. Avoid waterlogging ⌸ Tip cuttings

*Yucca elephantipes* 'Variegata' ▷
### VARIEGATED SPINELESS YUCCA
↕ 2.5m (8ft) ↔ 2m (6ft)

This popular and dramatic plant is also robust and ideal as a corner specimen. With age, the narrow, sword-shaped, cream-margined leaves will drop, revealing the yucca's characteristic bare stem.

☀ Bright, with some sun ☷ Moderate to warm, but cool in winter. Low humidity ♦ Fortnightly ◊ Keep moist. Water sparingly at low temperatures ⌸ Stem sections

SPECIFIC USES

# Beneficial Houseplants

Recent NASA research into the beneficial effects of plants has shown that they can significantly improve the indoor environment. Houseplants absorb carbon dioxide and breathe out oxygen, adding moisture to the air. They also alleviate "sick building syndrome" by removing airborne pollutants released by building materials, cleaners, and new furnishings. They really do promote a healthy, stress-free environment.

△ *Chlorophytum comosum*
'Mandaianum'
**Spider Plant**
↕ ↔ 60cm (2ft) or more

One of the most popular and easily grown houseplants, and an active remover of indoor pollution. Display it where its trailing habit can be seen.

☼ Bright to moderate, avoiding summer sun ≣ Moderate to warm. Moderate to high humidity ◊ Fortnightly. Stop if cool ◊ Keep moist. When dry if cool ▨ Plantlets

△ *Dieffenbachia seguine* 'Exotica'
**Dumb Cane**
↕ ↔ 90cm (3ft)

This air-pollutant-removing plant has spectacular, creamy-white variegated leaves. Their large size increases their absorbent capacity. Poisonous if chewed.

☼ Bright to moderate. Avoid hot sun ≣ Moderate to warm. Moderate to high humidity ◊ Fortnightly, using foliage houseplant fertilizer. Monthly in winter ◊ Water when dry ▨ Tip cuttings, stem sections

△ *Dracaena fragrans* 'Janet Craig'
**Dracaena**
↕ 3m (10ft) ↔ 1.2m (4ft)

A striking plant with erect stems and lush, glossy, dark green, strap-shaped leaves. The most effective dracaena form for absorbing chemical toxins from the air.

☼ Bright to moderate, avoiding hot sun ≣ Warm. Moderate to high humidity ◊ Fortnightly. Occasionally in winter ◊ Water when dry. Reduce at lower temperatures ▨ Tip cuttings, stem sections

△ *Ficus benjamina* 'Reginald'
**Weeping Fig**
↕ 3m (10ft) or more ↔ 1m (3ft) or more

Very effective at removing airborne chemicals, especially formaldehyde, the most common indoor pollutant. Its glossy green leaves are lime-green when young.

☼ Bright, but avoid summer sun ≣ Warm, avoiding fluctuation. Moderate to high humidity ◊ Fortnightly. Occasionally in winter ◊ When dry. Reduce watering in cool conditions ▨ Tip cuttings

---

**Other Beneficial Houseplants for Foliage Effect**

*Chamaedorea elegans*, see p.114
*Chlorophytum comosum* 'Vittatum', see p.86
*Chrysalidocarpus lutescens*, see p.114
*Dracaena marginata*, see p.97
*Epipremnum aureum*, see p.92
*Nephrolepis exaltata* 'Bostoniensis', see p.109
*Philodendron scandens* subsp. *oxycardium*
*Rhapis excelsa*, see p.115
*Syngonium podophyllum*

*Homalomena wallisii* ▷
**QUEEN OF HEARTS**
↕ ↔ 90cm (3ft)

The glossy, long-stalked, abruptly pointed foliage is particularly effective at removing ammonia, as well as other pollutants, from the air. A challenging plant to grow well.

☀ Moderate ⊫ Warm, but moderate in dormancy. Dislikes draughts. High humidity ◌ Fortnightly ◌ When compost surface just dry. Water sparingly in winter ✄ Division

---

**OTHER BENEFICIAL HOUSE-PLANTS FOR FLORAL EFFECT**

*Begonia* species and hybrids
*Chrysanthemum* hybrids
*Clivia miniata*, see p.28
*Gerbera jamesonii* cultivars
*Schlumbergera truncata*, see p.65
*Tulipa* hybrids, see p.103

---

△ *Ficus elastica* 'Robusta'
**RUBBER PLANT**
↕ 3m (10ft) or more ↔ 1.8m (6ft)

'Robusta', with its bold, glossy, leathery leaves, is one of the most handsome of the popular evergreen rubber plants. It is very effective at absorbing formaldehyde.

☀ Bright, but avoid summer sun ⊫ Warm. Moderate to high humidity ◌ Fortnightly. Occasionally in winter ◌ When dry. Reduce at lower temperatures ✄ Tip cuttings, air layering

◁ *Schefflera arboricola* 'Compacta'
**SCHEFFLERA**
↕ 1.8m (6ft) ↔ 90cm (3ft)

Compact in habit and erect-stemmed, this easy-to-grow evergreen produces masses of shining, deep green, fingered leaves. These will absorb chemical pollutants from the air.

☀ Bright to moderate ⊫ Moderate to warm, avoiding fluctuation. Moderate to high humidity ◌ Fortnightly. Monthly in winter ◌ Water when dry ✄ Division, tip cuttings, air layering

△ *Hedera helix* 'Green Ripple'
**COMMON IVY, ENGLISH IVY**
↕ 1m (3ft) or more ↔ 30cm (12in) or more

All ivies are efficient at removing air pollutants, but English ivy is particularly good at absorbing the formaldehyde that is found in tobacco smoke and adhesives.

☀ Bright to moderate. Poor growth in low light ⊫ Cool to moderate. Moderate to high humidity ◌ Fortnightly. Occasionally in winter ◌ When dry. Water sparingly in winter ✄ Tip cuttings, layering

△ *Spathiphyllum wallisii*
**PEACE LILY**
↕ ↔ 60cm (2ft)

An excellent capacity for absorbing acetone, benzene, and formaldehyde, and tolerance of low light, make this plant a winner. White spring and summer flowers.

☀ Bright, but avoid direct sun ⊫ Moderate to warm. Moderate to high humidity ◌ Fortnightly. Monthly in winter ◌ Water when compost dry. Avoid overwatering ✄ Division

# Trailing Houseplants

TRAILING PLANTS with lax stems are excellent subjects for hanging baskets, plinths, or high shelves. Some trail naturally, while others are young specimens of plants that are really climbers. Site trailers carefully so they have plenty of room to grow without being damaged and are easily accessible for watering.

## △ *Epipremnum aureum*
### DEVIL'S IVY
↕ 2m (6ft) ↔ 1m (3ft)

The young foliage of this handsome rainforest plant is bright green splashed with gold. Treat older plants as climbers. Easily controlled and propagated. ♉

☼ Bright, but avoid direct sun. Variegation fades in shade ▤ Moderate to warm. Moderate to high humidity ◐ Fortnightly. Twice in winter ◊ Water when compost surface dry ▭ Tip or stem cuttings

## *Aporocactus flagelliformis* f. *flagriformis* △
### RAT'S TAIL CACTUS
↕ ↔ 60cm (2ft)

In its native Mexico, this species hangs from trees, rock ledges, and crevices. It is excellent for a hanging basket, but should be sited away from walkways.

☼ Bright, but avoid direct sun ▤ Cool to warm. Moderate humidity ◐ Cactus and succulent feed every three weeks, spring to autumn ◊ When dry. Rarely in winter ▭ Division, stem cuttings, seed

### OTHER TRAILING HOUSEPLANTS

*Campanula isophylla*, see p.34
*Fuchsia* 'Golden Marinka'
*Glechoma hederacea* 'Variegata'
*Lotus maculatus*
*Oplismenus africanus* 'Variegatus'
*Rhipsalidopsis gaertneri*
*Sedum morganianum*, see p.111

## *Ceropegia linearis* subsp. *woodii* △
### ROSARY VINE
↕ 90cm (3ft) ↔ 10cm (4in)

This apparently delicate plant is surprisingly tough and can tolerate periods of drought. Pairs of marbled, heart-shaped, succulent leaves hang from the thread-like stems, often accompanied by fascinating slender, mauve-pink vase-shaped flowers. ♉

☼ Bright to moderate ▤ Cool to warm. Low humidity ◐ Fortnightly in summer, using high potash or cactus fertilizer ◊ When compost surface dry. Water sparingly in winter ▭ Tubers

## △ *Epipremnum* 'Neon'
### DEVIL'S IVY
↕ 2m (6ft) ↔ 1m (3ft)

Unusual lime-green leaves distinguish this devil's ivy, shown here when young. Initially a trailing plant, it produces climbing shoots after a year or two.

☼ Bright, but avoid direct sun. Colour fades in shade ▤ Moderate to warm. Moderate to high humidity ◐ Fortnightly. Twice in winter ◊ Water when compost surface dry ▭ Tip or stem cuttings

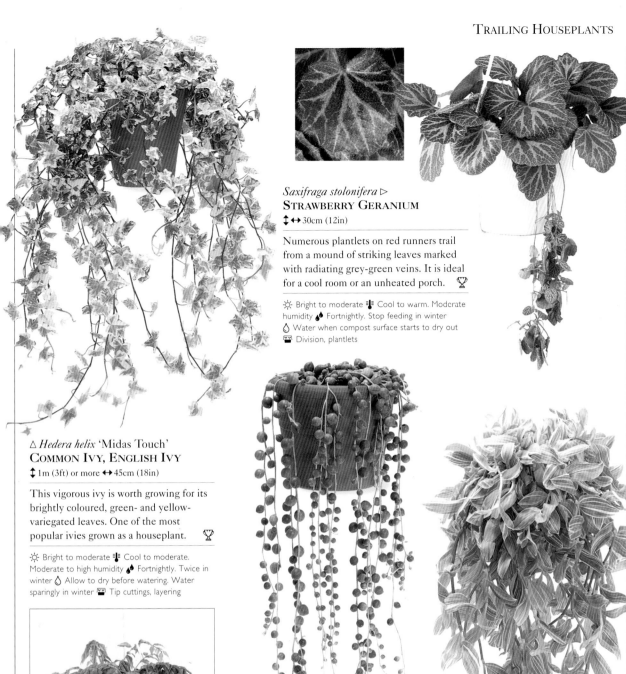

*Saxifraga stolonifera* ▷
**STRAWBERRY GERANIUM**

↕ ↔ 30cm (12in)

Numerous plantlets on red runners trail
from a mound of striking leaves marked
with radiating grey-green veins. It is ideal
for a cool room or an unheated porch. ♈

☼ Bright to moderate 🌡 Cool to warm. Moderate
humidity 🌢 Fortnightly. Stop feeding in winter
🌢 Water when compost surface starts to dry out
🗑 Division, plantlets

△ *Hedera helix* 'Midas Touch'
**COMMON IVY, ENGLISH IVY**

↕ 1m (3ft) or more ↔ 45cm (18in)

This vigorous ivy is worth growing for its
brightly coloured, green- and yellow-
variegated leaves. One of the most
popular ivies grown as a houseplant. ♈

☼ Bright to moderate 🌡 Cool to moderate.
Moderate to high humidity 🌢 Fortnightly. Twice in
winter 🌢 Allow to dry before watering. Water
sparingly in winter 🗑 Tip cuttings, layering

△ *Hoya lanceolata* subsp. *bella*
**MINIATURE WAX PLANT**

↕ ↔ 45cm (18in)

When the deliciously fragrant, waxy
flowers appear in summer, leave their
stalks, as buds will form on them for the
next display. Also grown as a climber. ♈

☼ Bright. Avoid direct sun 🌡 Moderate to warm.
Moderate to high humidity 🌢 Every three weeks,
using flowering houseplant fertilizer. Stop in winter
🌢 When dry. Rarely in winter 🗑 Tip cuttings

△ *Senecio rowleyanus*
**STRING OF BEADS**

↕ 1m (3ft) ↔ 8cm (3in)

A strange, succulent member of the daisy
family that produces a curtain of trailing
stems with pea-like leaves. Sweetly-
scented white flowers appear in autumn.

☼ Bright to moderate. Avoid summer sun 🌡 Cool
to warm. Low humidity 🌢 Every three weeks, using
high potash or cactus fertilizer. Stop in winter
🌢 Water when dry. Rarely in winter 🗑 Tip cuttings

△ *Tradescantia
fluminensis* 'Albovittata'
**INCH PLANT, WANDERING JEW**

↕ 1m (3ft) ↔ 15cm (6in)

Pure white flowers, borne in summer, add
interest to this fast-growing plant. Its lax
stems are clothed in fleshy, soft green
leaves, boldly marked with white stripes.

☼ Bright, but avoid summer sun. Variegation fades
in shade 🌡 Moderate to warm. Moderate to high
humidity 🌢 Fortnightly. Once in winter 🌢 Keep
moist. When dry if cool 🗑 Tip or stem cuttings

**SPECIFIC USES**

# Climbing Houseplants

MANY CLIMBERS are native to tropical rainforests, where they clamber up tree trunks and branches to reach the light. Large-leaved climbers need plenty of room in which to develop, but more slender varieties are ideal for tight corners or recesses. Climbers should be trained on a moss-clad frame or pole and pruned to size.

*Bougainvillea* 'Mrs. Butt' ▷
**BOUGAINVILLEA, PAPER FLOWER**
↕ ↔ 2m (6ft) or more

Deservedly popular in tropical gardens, this plant offers stunning, crimson-shaded magenta, papery bracts. Prune back the previous year's stems hard in midwinter.

☼ Bright, sunny ▮ Cool to warm. Moderate humidity ◐ Fortnightly, using flowering houseplant fertilizer. Stop feeding in winter ◊ Water when dry. Reduce in cool conditions ▧ Tip cuttings

*Monstera obliqua* ▷
**MONSTERA**
↕ 3m (10ft) or more ↔ 1.2m (4ft)

Highly perforated leaves give this bold climber an unusual shredded look. It is worth growing for novelty value alone; train up a moss pole or similar support.

☼ Bright to moderate ▮ Moderate to warm. Moderate to high humidity ◐ Fortnightly. Once in late autumn and once in midwinter ◊ Water when just dry ▧ Stem cuttings, air layering

△ *Cissus rhombifolia*
**GRAPE IVY**
↕ 3m (10ft) ↔ 60cm (2ft)

Boldly-toothed, glossy green leaflets cover this vigorous, tendrilled plant. Trained up canes or trellis, it will create an attractive living screen or room divider. ♔

☼ Bright, but avoid hot sun ▮ Moderate to warm. Moderate to high humidity ◐ Fortnightly, using foliage houseplant fertilizer. Monthly in winter ◊ Allow to dry before watering ▧ Tip cuttings

△ *Epipremnum aureum* 'Marble Queen'
**DEVIL'S IVY**
↕ 3m (10ft) ↔ 1m (3ft)

An outstanding climber with white-marbled foliage and white leaf stalks. The mass of eye-catching leaves is particularly distinctive when covering a moss pole.

☼ Bright, but avoid direct sun. Variegation fades in shade ▮ Moderate to warm. Moderate to high humidity ◐ Fortnightly. Twice in winter ◊ Water when dry ▧ Tip or stem cuttings

△ *Passiflora* 'Amethyst'
**PASSION FLOWER**
↕ ↔ 3m (10ft) or more

Vigorous even in cool climates, this plant has exotic flowers. If trained to a frame, prune long shoots to 1.5cm (½in) in spring and re-attach afterwards. Leave old wood.

☼ Bright, with some sun ▮ Moderate to warm. Moderate to high humidity ◐ Flowering houseplant fertilizer fortnightly. Stop in winter ◊ Water when dry. Keep just moist in winter ▧ Stem cuttings

*Philodendron* 'Medisa' ▷
**PHILODENDRON**
↕ 3m (10ft) ↔ 1m (3ft)

Red shoots and leaf stalks and
large leaves, golden yellow when
young, make this a very eye-catching
plant. A forest tree-climber in the wild, in
the home it thrives best on a moss pole.

☼ Bright to moderate, avoiding direct sun
🌡 Moderate to warm. Moderate to high humidity
💧 Fortnightly. Monthly in winter 💧 Water when
compost surface just dry ✂ Tip cuttings

---

### OTHER CLIMBING HOUSEPLANTS

*Cissus rhombifolia* 'Ellen Danica',
  see p.78
*Gelsemium sempervirens*
*Gloriosa superba* 'Rothschildiana'
*Hoya carnosa* 'Tricolor'
*Jasminum polyanthum*, see p.25
*Piper crocatum*
*Senecio mikanioides*
*Stephanotis floribunda* 'Alpine'
*Syngonium* 'Jenny'
*Tetrastigma voinierianum*

---

*Senecio macroglossus* 'Variegatus' ▷
**CAPE IVY, WAX VINE**
↕ 3m (10ft) ↔ 1m (3ft)

Looking like an ivy with yellow summer
and winter flowers, this daisy relative
climbs by twining stems, which can be
trained up canes or thin stakes.

☼ Bright, with some sun 🌡 Cool to warm.
Moderate humidity 💧 Fortnightly, from spring to
autumn 💧 When compost surface dry. Water
sparingly at low temperatures ✂ Tip cuttings

---

△ *Syngonium podophyllum* 'Imperial
White'
**GOOSEFOOT PLANT**
↕ 2m (6ft) or more ↔ 60cm (2ft)

Grow where the beautifully marked
leaves, which change shape as the plant
matures, can be appreciated. Climbing
stems may be pruned to retain bushiness.

☼ Bright to moderate, avoiding direct sun
🌡 Warm. Moderate to high humidity 💧 Fortnightly,
using foliage houseplant fertilizer. Monthly in winter
💧 When dry. Reduce in winter ✂ Tip cuttings

△ *Thunbergia alata*
**BLACK-EYED SUSAN**
↕ 2m (6ft) ↔ 30cm (12in)

This twining plant produces a display of
rich orange flowers with dark centres from
late spring to autumn, if deadheaded
regularly. Usually grown as an annual.

☼ Bright, with some sun 🌡 Moderate to warm.
Moderate humidity 💧 Fortnightly once established,
using flowering houseplant fertilizer 💧 Allow to dry
out before watering ✂ Seed

SPECIFIC USES

95

# Houseplants for Architectural Effect

NO PLANTS CONTRIBUTE more drama to the visual scheme of a room than those with large or deeply divided leaves or a striking habit. Careful siting is important if a plant's architectural qualities are to become a focal point. As a general rule, the bigger the plant and the space around it, the more effective its scale and form will appear.

*Araucaria heterophylla* ▷
**NORFOLK ISLAND PINE**
↕ 2.5m (8ft) or more ↔ 1.2m (4ft) or more

Like so many houseplants, this reaches a large size in its natural environment. Best grown indoors on a single stem, it is then less vigorous but still impressive. ♛

☼ Bright, but avoid summer sun ☖ Moderate. Moderate humidity ♦ Fortnightly. Occasionally in winter ♦ When compost surface dry. Water sparingly in winter ▨ Seed

△ *Beaucarnea recurvata*
**ELEPHANT'S FOOT, PONY TAIL**
↕ 1.8m (6ft) or more ↔ 1m (3ft) or more

An extraordinary-looking plant from Mexico that develops a bulbous base and a great topknot of slender, arching or pendulous leaves. Easy to grow. ♛

☼ Bright, with sun ☖ Moderate to warm. Low humidity ♦ Monthly, using fertilizer for cacti and succulents ♦ When compost surface dry. Water sparingly in winter ▨ Tip cuttings, offsets, seed

△ *Cycas revoluta*
**SAGO PALM**
↕ ↔ 1.5m (5ft)

This primitive evergreen, not a true palm, develops its short trunk very slowly, but the stiff, leathery, deeply divided leaves are spectacular even on a young plant. ♛

☼ Bright, but avoid direct summer sun ☖ Warm. Moderate to high humidity ♦ Monthly ♦ Water when compost surface dry ▨ Seed, buds from old or dormant plants

△ *Dracaena fragrans* 'White Stripe'
**DRACAENA**
↕ 2m (6ft) or more ↔ 1m (3ft)

A striking foliage plant producing stiffly erect stems and generous clusters of long, pointed green leaves, with white-striped margins. This is a bold specimen plant.

☼ Bright to moderate, avoiding summer sun ☖ Warm. Moderate to high humidity ♦ Fortnightly. Occasionally in winter ♦ When dry. Water sparingly in winter ▨ Tip cuttings, stem sections

---

**OTHER NARROW-LEAVED ARCHITECTURAL HOUSEPLANTS**

*Cordyline australis*
*Dracaena draco*
*Pandanus veitchii*, see p.43
*Phormium tenax*
*Sansevieria trifasciata*, see p.89
*Yucca elephantipes*, see p.87

### *Dracaena marginata* ▷
### MADAGASCAR DRAGON TREE

↕ 3m (10ft) ↔ 1.2m (4ft)

Bold tufts of shining, grassy, red-edged green leaves bring a touch of the exotic to any room. This native of Madagascar is one of the most popular dracaenas for indoor cultivation. ♕

☼ Bright to moderate, avoiding summer sun ❄ Warm. Moderate to high humidity ♦ Fortnightly. Occasionally in winter ♦ When dry. Sparingly in winter ✂ Tip cuttings, stem sections

### *Schefflera arboricola* 'Gold Capella' ▷
### SCHEFFLERA

↕ 1.8m (6ft) ↔ 1m (3ft)

The umbrella tree is grown as a houseplant for its long-stalked juvenile foliage, which is divided into rich green, gold-splashed leaflets. A dark background or group setting is effective. ♕

☼ Bright to moderate ❄ Warm, avoiding fluctuation. Moderate to high humidity ♦ Fortnightly. Monthly in winter ♦ Water when compost surface dry ✂ Tip cuttings, air layering

*Large, feather-shaped fronds*

### △ *Ficus lyrata*
### BANJO FIG, FIDDLE-LEAF FIG

↕ 3m (10ft) or more ↔ 1.8m (6ft) or more

Give this plant plenty of elbow room to accommodate its likely spread and show off its spectacular large, waisted leaves. This fig originates in African forests. ♕

☼ Bright. Avoid summer sun ❄ Warm. Moderate to high humidity ♦ Fortnightly. Occasionally in winter ♦ When compost surface dry. Reduce at lower temperatures ✂ Tip cuttings, air layering

### △ *Lytocaryum weddellianum*
### DWARF COCONUT PALM

↕ 2m (6ft) ↔ 1.5m (5ft)

One of the most beautiful palms for the home and tolerant of low light. Handle the fragile roots with care when repotting. Formerly sold as *Microcoelum* or *Cocos*. ♕

☼ Moderate to shady ❄ Warm. Moderate to high humidity ♦ Every three weeks ♦ When compost surface dry. Water sparingly in winter. Avoid waterlogging ✂ Seed

### △ *Schefflera elegantissima* 'Castor'
### FALSE ARALIA, FINGER ARALIA

↕ 2m (6ft) ↔ 90cm (3ft)

This plant produces an elegant, lacy outline. The dark coppery-green leaves have long, narrow leaflets that widen with age. Also known as *Aralia* or *Dizygotheca*.

☼ Bright, avoiding direct sun ❄ Warm, avoiding fluctuation. Moderate humidity ♦ Fortnightly. Monthly at low winter temperatures ♦ Water when dry. Avoid overwatering ✂ Tip cuttings, seed

# Houseplants with Ornamental Fruit

HOUSEPLANTS WORTH growing for their fruits alone are in the minority, yet they include some very reliable and colourful varieties. Some of these are seasonal plants, and useful for adding winter interest. They include capsicums, winter cherries, and hardy plants such as *Aucuba* and *Skimmia*. The fruits shown here are inedible, but not poisonous unless stated.

*Ardisia crenata* ▷
## CORAL BERRY
↕ 1m (3ft) ↔ 30cm (12in) or more

Chiefly grown for its colourful red berries, freely borne especially in winter, this evergreen has glossy, toothed leaves. Prune in early spring after berries finish.

☼ Bright, but avoid direct sun ❄ Moderate. Moderate to high humidity ◈ Monthly. Occasionally in winter ◊ When compost surface dry. Reduce watering in winter ✂ Semi-ripe cuttings, seed

SPECIFIC USES

*Capsicum annuum* ▷
## CHRISTMAS PEPPER
↕ 30cm (12in)
↔ 30cm (12in) or more

Commonly available in winter, this well-known houseplant is popular for its usually conical, some-times rounded, red or yellow, long-lasting fruits. It is usually treated as an annual pot plant.

☼ Bright ❄ Cool to moderate. Moderate humidity ◈ Every week, alternating general fertilizer with flowering houseplant fertilizer ◊ Water when compost surface just dry ✂ Seed

*Capsicum annuum*
'Festival Orange' △
## ORNAMENTAL PEPPER
↕ ↔ 60cm (2ft)

In winter, this colourful houseplant produces conical, bright orange, long-lasting fruits, strikingly set among the dark green foliage. It will enjoy a position on a sunny windowsill.

☼ Bright, but avoid direct sun ❄ Cool to moderate. Moderate humidity ◈ Fortnightly, alternating general fertilizer with flowering houseplant fertilizer ◊ Water when compost surface just dry ✂ Tip cuttings

OTHER HOUSEPLANTS WITH
ORNAMENTAL FRUIT

*Aechmea fulgens* var. *discolor*
*Ananas bracteatus* 'Tricolor', see p.60
*Ardisia crispa*
*Capsicum annuum* 'Masquerade'
    *Fuchsia procumbens*
        *Nertera balfouriana*
            *Punica granatum* var. *nana*

x *Citrofortunella microcarpa* ▷
## CALAMONDIN
↕ ↔ 1.2m (4ft)

Miniature oranges, 3–4cm (1¼–1½in) across, make this shrub an attractive houseplant; the fruits are produced at almost any time, even by young plants, but are bitter to the taste.

☼ Bright, but avoid summer sun ❄ Moderate to warm. Moderate to high humidity ◈ Fortnightly, using fertilizer for ericaceous plants. Monthly in winter ◊ Water when compost surface dry ✂ Semi-ripe cuttings

*Rhipsalis floccosa* ▷
**MISTLETOE CACTUS**

↕ 45cm (18in) ↔ 24cm (10in)

In spring, mistletoe-like white, sometimes
pink-tinted berries are produced on the
long, slender stems of this curious
weeping cactus. Good for a hanging pot.

☼ Bright ▮ Moderate to warm, with cool winter
rest. Moderate to high humidity ⬤ Monthly, using
flowering houseplant fertilizer. Occasionally in winter
⬤ When dry. Sparingly in winter ▭ Stem sections

Long-lasting
fruits

*Skimmia
japonica*
'Robert Fortune' ▷
**SKIMMIA**

↕ 60cm (2ft) ↔ 1m (3ft)

Slow-growing, and
usually low-growing
when cultivated as a houseplant,
this evergreen shrub is a popular
choice for its dense clusters of long-
lasting, dark red fruits, borne from
summer through to winter.

☼ Moderate to shady ▮ Cool to moderate.
Moderate humidity ⬤ Fortnightly ⬤ When
compost surface just dry. Reduce watering in winter
▭ Semi-ripe cuttings

△ *Fortunella japonica*
**ROUND KUMQUAT**

↕ 3m (10ft) or more ↔ 1.5m (5ft) or more

Edible, golden-orange fruits, lasting
throughout autumn, are produced by this
thorny shrub; fragrant white flowers
appear in spring. Closely related to *Citrus*.

☼ Bright, but avoid summer sun ▮ Moderate to
warm. Moderate to high humidity ⬤ Fortnightly,
using fertilizer for ericaceous plants. Monthly in
winter ⬤ Keep moist ▭ Semi-ripe cuttings

△ *Nertera granadensis*
**BEAD PLANT, CORAL MOSS**

↕ 2cm (¾in) ↔ 20cm (8in)

The moss-like, emerald-green cushion or
mat of slender, prostrate, interlacing stems
is studded with orange berries in autumn.
An irresistible plant for a windowsill.

☼ Bright. Avoid summer sun ▮ Cool to moderate.
Moderate to high humidity ⬤ Monthly. Occasionally
in winter ⬤ When compost surface dry. Water
sparingly in winter ▭ Division, tip cuttings, seed

### OTHER HARDY HOUSEPLANTS WITH ORNAMENTAL FRUIT

*Arbutus unedo* 'Elfin King'
*Aucuba japonica* 'Rozannie'
*Duchesnea indica*, see p.66
*Gaultheria procumbens*
*Pyracantha coccinea* 'Red Column'
*Vaccinium vitis-idaea* 'Koralle'

◁ *Solanum pseudocapsicum*
**JERUSALEM CHERRY**

↕ ↔ 60cm (2ft)

The large, spherical, winter fruits of this
plant are orange-red, bright red when ripe,
and decorative but poisonous. Generally
grown as an annual in the winter season.

☼ Bright, but avoid direct sun ▮ Cool to
moderate. Moderate humidity ⬤ Fortnightly, alternating general fertilizer with flowering houseplant
fertilizer ⬤ Water when just dry ▭ Tip cuttings

# Houseplants for Terraria

THESE CLOSED GLASS containers can be home to miniature gardens or jungles. They are draught-free and provide constant humidity and warmth, which allows a good range of interesting and ornamental plants, even "difficult" varieties, to flourish. Reasonably easy to look after, they make a distinctive focal point.

△ *Hypoestes phyllostachya*
**POLKA DOT PLANT**
↕ 30cm (12in) ↔ 23cm (9in)

Pinch out the slender spikes of small flowers to preserve the effect of the pale-pink-spotted leaves. For a compact habit, also pinch out the growing tips.

☼ Bright, but avoid summer sun ⬍ Warm. Moderate to high humidity ◐ Fortnightly. Occasionally in winter ◊ Water when compost surface just dry ▨ Tip cuttings. Roots easily in water

*Adiantum raddianum* ▷
**DELTA MAIDENHAIR FERN**
↕ 60cm (2ft) ↔ 80cm (32in)

A mound of loosely arching, delicately divided fronds, borne on slender, wiry, shining black stalks, is produced by this elegant fern from tropical South America.

☼ Moderate, avoiding direct sun ⬍ Moderate to warm. Moderate to high humidity ◐ Fortnightly. Monthly in winter ◊ Keep moist, but avoid waterlogging ▨ Division, spores

△ *Hypoestes phyllostachya*
'Vinrod'
**POLKA DOT PLANT**
↕ 30cm (12in) ↔ 23cm (9in)

The rich wine-red leaves, marked with contrasting pink splashes, are a showy alternative to the typical polka dot plant. Keep it compact by pinching out the growing tips and flower spikes.

☼ Bright, but avoid summer sun ⬍ Warm. Moderate to high humidity ◐ Fortnightly. Occasionally in winter ◊ Water when compost surface just dry ▨ Tip cuttings. Roots easily in water

△ *Episcia cupreata*
**FLAME VIOLET**
↕ 15cm (6in) ↔ 30cm (12in)

A creeping, mat-forming perennial from the Amazon, with attractive leaves, purple beneath and pale-veined above. The red flowers appear throughout summer.

☼ Bright to moderate, avoiding direct sun ⬍ Warm. High humidity ◐ Fortnightly. Occasionally in winter ◊ When compost surface just dry. Avoid waterlogging ▨ Division, tip cuttings

△ *Fittonia verschaffeltii* var. *argyroneura*
'Mini White'
**SILVER NET LEAF**
↕ 10cm (4in) ↔ 30cm (12in)

This choice creeping and carpeting perennial from the rainforests of Peru has exquisitely silver-veined green leaves. A "must" for any terrarium or bottle garden.

☼ Moderate to shady, avoiding direct sun ⬍ Warm. High humidity ◐ Fortnightly. Occasionally in winter ◊ Keep moist, but avoid waterlogging ▨ Tip cuttings

**OTHER FLOWERING HOUSEPLANTS FOR TERRARIA**

*Episcia* 'Cleopatra'
*Episcia lilacina*
*Episcia* 'Pink Panther'
*Peperomia fraseri*
*Saintpaulia* 'Blue Imp'
*Saintpaulia* 'Pip Squeek', see p.39
*Streptocarpus saxorum*, see p.39

## △ *Maranta leuconeura* var. *erythroneura*
### RED HERRINGBONE PLANT
↕ 25cm (10in) ↔ 30cm (12in) or more

One of the most beautiful and striking foliage plants, from the rainforests of Brazil. Red herringbone plants form mats of large, pale green leaves, with darker zones and red veins.

☼ Moderate, avoiding direct sun ⬛ Warm. Moderate to high humidity 💧 Fortnightly. Occasionally in winter ◌ Keep moist, but avoid waterlogging. In winter, water when compost surface just dry ⬒ Division, tip cuttings

## △ *Pilea involucrata* 'Moon Valley'
### FRIENDSHIP PLANT, PILEA
↕ ↔ 30cm (12in)

This trailing or creeping plant must be seen to be believed. The pale green leaves are remarkably puckered and have a network of sunken red veins. Well worth growing in a small terrarium or bell jar.

☼ Bright to moderate, with some sun ⬛ Warm. Moderate to high humidity 💧 Every three weeks. Occasionally in winter ◌ Water when compost surface just dry. Avoid waterlogging ⬒ Tip cuttings

## △ *Pilea cadierei* 'Minima'
### ALUMINIUM PLANT
↕ ↔ 15cm (6in)

A compact form of *P. cadierei* (see p.55), with similar silver and green puckered leaves. It makes a striking specimen in a small terrarium or bell jar; in larger terraria it mixes well with green-leaved companions.

☼ Bright to moderate, with some sun ⬛ Warm. Moderate to high humidity 💧 Every three weeks. Occasionally in winter ◌ Water when compost surface just dry. Avoid waterlogging ⬒ Tip cuttings

## △ *Peperomia obtusifolia* 'Greengold'
### DESERT PRIVET
↕ ↔ 25cm (10in)

Erect stems and big, fleshy, creamy-yellow leaves variegated with irregular dark and pale green centres make this bushy plant spectacular when well grown.

☼ Bright to moderate, with some sun ⬛ Warm. Moderate to high humidity 💧 Every three weeks. Occasionally in winter ◌ When compost surface just dry. Avoid waterlogging ⬒ Tip cuttings

### OTHER FOLIAGE HOUSEPLANTS FOR TERRARIA

*Bertolonia marmorata*
*Ficus pumila* 'White Sonny', see p.65
*Peperomia caperata* 'Little Fantasy'
*Peperomia marmorata*
*Pilea involucrata* 'Norfolk'
*Pilea repens*
*Selaginella martensii*, see p.67
*Selaginella uncinata*
*Sonerila margaritacea* 'Hendersonii'

## △ *Selaginella kraussiana* 'Aurea'
### SPREADING CLUBMOSS
↕ 2.5cm (1in) ↔ indefinite

This easy-to-grow fern relative produces rapidly forking, slender stems, densely crowded with tiny, yellow-green, scale-like leaves. May need reducing in size.

☼ Shady ⬛ Warm. High humidity 💧 Every five weeks, using half-strength general houseplant fertilizer ◌ Water when compost surface just dry. Avoid waterlogging ⬒ Stem cuttings

101

# Dual-purpose Houseplants

AN INCREASING NUMBER of winter-hardy plants are grown indoors; they include foliage plants for rooms with low heat, but more commonly are flowering and bulbous plants for temporary display. So often these "one-off" plants are thrown away after their flowering season is over, when in fact they can be planted in the garden, and left to flower and be enjoyed in future years.

△ *Iris reticulata*
**MINIATURE IRIS**
↕ 15cm (6in) ↔ 8cm (3in)

Planted in early autumn, this bulb bears fragrant flowers in late winter. Charming for a well-lit windowsill; plant out in a bed or rock garden in the autumn. ♈

☼ Bright to moderate, with some sun ⧟ Cool to moderate. Moderate humidity ♦ Fortnightly ♦ Water sparingly, increase as growth appears, keep moist, and reduce as leaves die ▦ Division

*Aster* 'Speedy Ruby Red' ▷
**MICHAELMAS DAISY**
↕ 30cm (12in) ↔ 45cm (18in)

One of several excellent dwarf Michaelmas daisies, with a compact habit and reddish flowers. This plant will give a reliable early autumn display in a cool room, and is easy to divide in spring.

☼ Bright, but avoid direct sun ⧟ Moderate. Moderate humidity ♦ Every three weeks ♦ Keep moist, but avoid waterlogging ▦ Division, tip cuttings

◁ *Astilbe* 'Deutschland'
**ASTILBE**
↕ 50cm (20in) ↔ 30cm (12in)

Like many astilbes, this one is commonly forced to flower in early spring. It offers a lovely combination of ferny foliage and splendid, erect, plumed white flowers.

☼ Bright, with some sun ⧟ Cool to moderate, with a cool winter rest. Moderate humidity ♦ Fortnightly feed ♦ Keep moist ▦ Division

— *Dark green ferny foliage*

△ *Muscari armeniacum*
**GRAPE HYACINTH**
↕ 20cm (8in) ↔ 5cm (2in)

In autumn, plant in a pot or pan to enjoy the sight of this cheerful-looking, blue-flowered bulb in spring. Planted outside in sun, it will naturalize in time. ♈

☼ Bright to moderate, with some sun ⧟ Cool to moderate. Moderate humidity ♦ Fortnightly ♦ Water sparingly; increase as growth appears; keep moist; reduce as leaves die ▦ Division, offsets

**OTHER DUAL-PURPOSE HOUSEPLANTS**

*Convallaria majalis* 'Fortin's Giant'
*Erica carnea* 'Winter Beauty'
*Helleborus niger* Blackthorn Group
*Passiflora caerulea*
*Primula* Polyanthus Group
*Tolmiea menziesii* 'Taff's Gold', see p.79

SPECIFIC USES

102

*Narcissus* hybrids ▷
## DAFFODIL
↕ 45cm (18in) ↔ 10cm (4in)

Most, if not all, daffodils make splendid flowering pot plants. Planted in autumn and forced, they can be flowering indoors as early as late winter. Plant them outside the following autumn.

☼ Bright to moderate, with some sun ❄ Cool to moderate. Moderate humidity ♦ Fortnightly ♦ Water sparingly; increase as growth appears; keep moist; reduce as leaves die ▦ Division, offsets

△ *Puschkinia scilloides*
## PUSCHKINIA
↕ 15cm (6in) ↔ 5cm (2in)

An excellent subject for a windowsill in a cool room, it should be planted in a pot in autumn for spring flowering. Afterwards, dry off, store, and plant out in autumn.

☼ Bright to moderate, with some sun ❄ Cool to moderate. Moderate humidity ♦ Fortnightly ♦ Water sparingly, increase as growth appears, keep moist in full growth, and reduce as leaves die ▦ Division, offsets

△ *Oxalis tetraphylla* 'Iron Cross'
## GOOD LUCK PLANT, LUCKY CLOVER
↕ 25cm (10in) ↔ 15cm (6in)

Easily recognizable by its dark purple leaf markings; the flowers appear in summer. It is not fully hardy in cold climates, so plant out in a sunny, well-drained spot.

☼ Bright, with some sun ❄ Moderate to warm, but cool in winter. Moderate humidity ♦ Fortnightly ♦ When compost surface dry. Water sparingly in winter ▦ Division, offsets

◁ *Tulipa* hybrids
## TULIP
↕ 60cm (2ft) ↔ 50cm (20in)

An enormous array of tulips is available for indoor use; they enjoy cool rather than heated rooms. After they flower in winter and spring, dry off, store, and plant them outside in the autumn.

☼ Bright to moderate, with some sun ❄ Cool to moderate. Moderate humidity ♦ Fortnightly ♦ Water sparingly, increase as growth appears, keep moist in growth, and reduce as leaves die ▦ Division, offsets

*Bold flowers available in many colours*

◁ *Primula vulgaris*
## PRIMROSE
↕ 15cm (6in)
↔ 20cm (8in)

A neat habit and large, velvety flowers, produced in winter and spring, mark out this familiar perennial. Cultivars and hybrids are sold in many colours. After it has finished flowering, plant outside in a border or bed.

☼ Bright to moderate, avoiding direct sun ❄ Cool to moderate. Moderate humidity ♦ Fortnightly. Monthly in winter ♦ Water when compost surface just dry ▦ Seed

### OTHER BULBOUS DUAL-PURPOSE HOUSEPLANTS

*Crocus chrysanthus*
*Cyclamen coum*
*Galanthus* 'Atkinsii'
*Hyacinthus orientalis* hybrids, see p.25
*Scilla siberica*

SPECIFIC USES

# Herbs for the Kitchen

WHERE BETTER TO GROW the herbs you need for cooking than in your kitchen, giving you a constant fresh supply that is immediately to hand? There is a wide range of easy-to-grow herbs suitable for cultivating indoors. Grow them in pots on a window ledge and snip regularly to keep them at a small size. Replace any exhausted plants when necessary.

*Allium schoenoprasum* ▷
## CHIVES
↕ ↔ 15cm (6in) or more

A favourite perennial herb for use in salads, this slender bulbous plant will soon form a clump but should not be allowed to flower. Snip off the decorative flower-heads (see inset) if they appear.

☼ Moderate ⬛ Moderate, but cool in winter. Moderate humidity ◖ Fortnightly ◌ When compost surface dry. Water sparingly in winter ⬚ Division, seed (let flower if seed required)

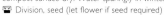

△ *Mentha spicata* 'Crispa'
## CURLY SPEARMINT
↕ ↔ 15cm (6in) or more

Crinkly leaves mark this form of the most popular and commonly cultivated garden mint. It is very vigorous, but can be kept to a manageable size by regular snipping.

☼ Bright, with some direct sun ⬛ Moderate to warm. Moderate humidity ◖ Occasional feed ◌ Keep consistently moist. Water sparingly in winter ⬚ Division

*Laurus nobilis* ▷
## BAY TREE
↕ 60cm (2ft) or more ↔ 30cm (12in) or more

This well-known evergreen grows into a large bush or small tree in the garden, but can easily be kept at a convenient size by regular pinching of the growing tips. ♈

☼ Bright, with some sun ⬛ Moderate. Moderate humidity ◖ Occasional feed ◌ Water when compost surface dry. Sparingly in winter ⬚ Semi-ripe cuttings

△ *Mentha* x *piperita*
## BLACK PEPPERMINT
↕ ↔ 15cm (6in) or more

Hardy, fast-creeping and clump-forming, with dark stems and fragrant green leaves, this perennial is easily controlled by pinching. Use in teas to aid digestion.

☼ Bright, with some direct sun ⬛ Moderate to warm. Moderate humidity ◖ Occasional feed ◌ Keep moist. Water sparingly in winter ⬚ Division

△ *Ocimum basilicum*
## SWEET BASIL
↕ ↔ 15cm (6in) or more

Strongly clove-scented leaves from this annual or short-lived perennial give a spicy flavour to salads and other foods. Pinch out the flowers as they appear.

☼ Bright, with some direct sun ⬛ Warm. Moderate humidity ◖ Fortnightly, using foliage houseplant fertilizer ◌ Water when compost surface dry ⬚ Seed

△ *Origanum vulgare*
**OREGANO, WILD MARJORAM**
↕ ↔ 15cm (6in) or more

The pungent, peppery-flavoured leaves of this bushy, woody-based perennial are used in bouquet garni. Chew the leaves to gain temporary relief from toothache.

☼ Bright ≣ Moderate to warm. Moderate humidity
♦ Occasional feed ◊ When compost surface dry.
Water sparingly in winter ⊞ Division, semi-ripe cuttings, seed

△ *Petroselinum crispum*
**CURLED PARSLEY**
↕ ↔ 15cm (6in)

Commonly grown, this bushy biennial herb has congested clusters of emerald-green crispy foliage and is popular as a flavouring or garnish. Treat as annual. ♛

☼ Bright to moderate, avoiding direct sun ≣ Low to moderate. Moderate humidity ♦ Fortnightly feed
◊ Keep consistently moist. Reduce watering in winter ⊞ Seed

---

**OTHER HERBS FOR THE KITCHEN**

*Anethum graveolens* (dill)
*Anthriscus cerefolium* (chervil)
*Artemisia dracunculus* (French tarragon)
*Coriandrum sativum* (coriander)
*Cymbopogon citratus* (lemon grass)
*Origanum majorana* (sweet marjoram)
*Rumex scutatus* (French sorrel)
*Sanguisorba minor* (salad burnet)

---

△ *Rosmarinus officinalis* 'Prostratus'
**PROSTRATE ROSEMARY**
↕ 15cm (6in) ↔ 30cm (12in) or more

A low-growing, spreading form of the popular rosemary, whose aromatic leaves flavour shellfish, pork, and lamb. Blue flowers appear in spring and summer. ♛

☼ Bright ≣ Moderate to warm. Moderate humidity
♦ Occasional feed ◊ Water when compost surface dry. In winter, water sparingly ⊞ Semi-ripe cuttings, layering

△ *Salvia officinalis*
**COMMON SAGE**
↕ ↔ 30cm (12in) or more

Pinch out the tips of this evergreen subshrub regularly to maintain a compact habit. Its pungent leaves are used for stuffing poultry and flavouring meat.

☼ Bright ≣ Moderate to warm. Moderate humidity
♦ Occasional feed ◊ Water when compost surface dry. Water sparingly in winter ⊞ Tip or semi-ripe cuttings, layering, seed

---

△ *Thymus* x *citriodorus* 'Aureus'
**LEMON-SCENTED THYME**
↕ 15cm (6in) or more ↔ 20cm (8in)

This pretty, bushy, evergreen shrublet is densely clothed in tiny, gold-dappled, lemon-scented leaves; an excellent herb that is both useful and ornamental. ♛

☼ Bright ≣ Moderate to warm. Moderate humidity
♦ Feed only if growth poor and leaves yellow
◊ Water when compost surface dry ⊞ Division, tip or semi-ripe cuttings

△ *Thymus vulgaris*
**COMMON THYME**
↕ 15cm (6in) ↔ 25cm (10in)

Thyme is commonly used in bouquet garni and as a flavouring for soups and stews. A dense evergreen shrublet, of spreading habit, it has tiny green leaves.

☼ Bright ≣ Moderate to warm. Moderate humidity
♦ Feed only if growth poor and leaves yellow
◊ Water when compost surface dry ⊞ Division, semi-ripe cuttings, seed

# SPECIALIST PLANTS

COLLECTING MEMBERS of a particular plant family or group is a satisfying and challenging way of growing houseplants. Although members of a family may be botanically related, they often differ greatly in appearance as well as in their individual cultivation requirements.

△ LONG-LASTING ORCHID *The long life of these large heads of delicately coloured orchid blooms adds to their appeal.*

Succulent *Aeonium* 'Zwartkop' for special interest

The popularity of some specialist plant collections may lie in the challenge of growing "difficult" plants. However, as well as those that demand skill and experience, there are houseplant groups that are fairly easy to grow, offering gardeners – especially beginners – the encouragement they need.

## SELECTING A PLANT GROUP

There are several factors to bear in mind when choosing a family or group of plants to collect. Beyond personal preference, there are the questions of facilities and space. Not every home can provide the different levels of temperature, light, and humidity required by, say, humidity-loving bromeliads and shade-loving ferns. Some groups require large amounts of space; palms, for example, are not suitable for a small room. It is little wonder that cacti and succulents, with their abundance of dwarf or compact, easy-to-grow species have proved such favourites: they can be comfortably contained on a sunny windowsill or similar position.

Some groups, such as the huge orchid family, offer a wide variety of flower form, colour, or both. For successful orchid cultivation, bear in mind that some are epiphytes, growing on trees and rocks in the wild, while some are terrestrial, rooting in the ground. There is also an extensive range of plants with curious or even abnormal growth habits or foliage, which can make an interesting and unusual collection.

◁ FERN COLLECTION *Making the most of a cool, shady wall, this magnificent group of adiantum, asplenium, and nephrolepis displays the variety of leaf textures and growth habits to great effect.*

▷ BRIGHT BROMELIAD *The bold-coloured flowerheads of most bromeliads make them eminently collectable. A warm kitchen provides the perfect opportunity to grow a range of these plants.*

# Ferns for Special Interest

A GROUP OF FERNS is one of the most fascinating and satisfying of plant collections because of their great variety, lush foliage, and their acceptance of less than perfect growing conditions. Few plants are more tolerant of low light, and while those of rainforest or tropical origin require warmth and high humidity if they are to thrive, there are many varieties that enjoy cooler conditions or even an unheated room.

△ *Didymochlaena truncatula*
**CLOAK FERN**
‡ 1.2m (4ft) ↔ 90cm (3ft)

A large but graceful plant when mature, the cloak fern is prized for its shining green, deeply divided fronds, tinted rosy-pink when young. Develops a short stem.

☼ Moderate to shady, avoiding summer sun
❄️ Moderate to warm. High humidity 💧 Fortnightly. Occasionally in winter 💧 Keep moist, but avoid waterlogging. Reduce in winter 🗺 Division, spores

*Adiantum* 'Bicolor' ▷
**MAIDENHAIR FERN**
‡ ↔ 30cm (12in)

One of many lovely adiantums, with the elegant characteristics of its relatives including beautifully divided emerald-green fronds. A bathroom window is ideal for this plant.

☼ Moderate to shady, avoiding direct sun
❄️ Moderate to warm, avoiding draughts. Moderate to high humidity 💧 Fortnightly. Monthly in winter
💧 Keep moist 🗺 Division, spores

△ *Asplenium nidus*
**BIRD'S NEST FERN**
‡ ↔ 90cm (3ft)

Named for its large shuttlecocks or clumps of bold, glossy green fronds, this tropical fern can be very tolerant of home conditions. Excellent for bathrooms. 🏆

☼ Moderate. Avoid direct sun ❄️ Warm, avoiding fluctuation and draughts. Moderate to high humidity 💧 Fortnightly, using foliage houseplant fertilizer. Occasionally in winter 💧 Keep moist 🗺 Spores

*Blechnum gibbum* ▷
**DWARF TREE FERN**
‡ 75cm (30in) ↔ 60cm (2ft)

This handsome fern from Fiji and New Caledonia develops a fine crown of deeply and regularly divided, leathery fronds. In time, the dwarf tree fern forms a short, densely scaly false stem.

☼ Bright to shady, avoiding direct sun ❄️ Moderate to warm. High humidity 💧 Fortnightly. Occasionally in winter 💧 Water when compost surface dry 🗺 Spores

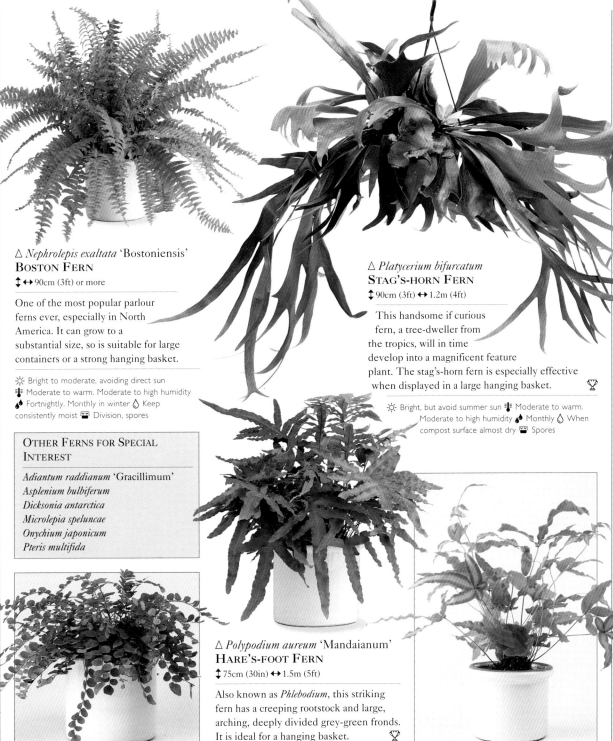

△ *Nephrolepis exaltata* 'Bostoniensis'
**BOSTON FERN**
↕ ↔ 90cm (3ft) or more

One of the most popular parlour ferns ever, especially in North America. It can grow to a substantial size, so is suitable for large containers or a strong hanging basket.

☼ Bright to moderate, avoiding direct sun
⬙ Moderate to warm. Moderate to high humidity
💧 Fortnightly. Monthly in winter ◊ Keep consistently moist ▭ Division, spores

### OTHER FERNS FOR SPECIAL INTEREST

*Adiantum raddianum* 'Gracillimum'
*Asplenium bulbiferum*
*Dicksonia antarctica*
*Microlepia speluncae*
*Onychium japonicum*
*Pteris multifida*

△ *Pellaea rotundifolia*
**BUTTON FERN**
↕ 20cm (8in) ↔ 30cm (12in)

Tolerant of brighter light than most ferns, this New Zealand plant forms a loose hummock of hairy, deeply divided fronds. It is ideal for growing in a small pot. ♈

☼ Moderate, avoiding direct sun ⬙ Moderate. High humidity 💧 Fortnightly. Monthly feed in winter ◊ Keep moist, but avoid waterlogging ▭ Division, spores

△ *Polypodium aureum* 'Mandaianum'
**HARE'S-FOOT FERN**
↕ 75cm (30in) ↔ 1.5m (5ft)

Also known as *Phlebodium*, this striking fern has a creeping rootstock and large, arching, deeply divided grey-green fronds. It is ideal for a hanging basket. ♈

☼ Bright to moderate, avoiding direct sun
⬙ Moderate to warm. Moderate to high humidity
💧 Monthly ◊ Keep moist, but avoid waterlogging
▭ Rhizomes, spores

### OTHER FERNS FOR HANGING BASKETS

*Adiantum diaphanum*
*Davallia canariensis*
*Davallia mariesii*
*Goniophlebium biauriculatum*
*Platycerium superbum*

△ *Platycerium bifurcatum*
**STAG'S-HORN FERN**
↕ 90cm (3ft) ↔ 1.2m (4ft)

This handsome if curious fern, a tree-dweller from the tropics, will in time develop into a magnificent feature plant. The stag's-horn fern is especially effective when displayed in a large hanging basket. ♈

☼ Bright, but avoid summer sun ⬙ Moderate to warm. Moderate to high humidity 💧 Monthly ◊ When compost surface almost dry ▭ Spores

△ *Pteris cretica* 'Albolineata'
**VARIEGATED TABLE FERN**
↕ 45cm (18in) ↔ 60cm (2ft)

An impressive fern with loose clumps of erect then arching, deeply divided fronds, whose narrow-fingered lobes have a bold stripe along the midrib. Easy to grow. ♈

☼ Bright, but avoid direct sun ⬙ Warm. Moderate to high humidity 💧 Fortnightly. Monthly in winter ◊ Keep moist, but avoid waterlogging ▭ Division, spores

# Cacti and Succulents for Special Interest

RELATIVELY EASY to grow, cacti and succulents introduce many people, especially children, to the world of plants. Most enjoy or will tolerate dry air, although this is no reason to neglect them. Curious growth forms and colourful flowers are among their specialities.

*Aeonium* 'Zwartkop' ▷
**BLACK AEONIUM**
↕ ↔ 90cm (3ft)

A dramatic plant that slowly grows into a succulent "tree" with bold rosettes of shining, blackish-purple leaves. Large heads of yellow flowers appear in spring or early summer.

☼ Bright, with direct sun ◱ Warm, but cool to moderate in winter. Low humidity ◖ Monthly, using fertilizer for cacti and succulents ◊ When compost surface dry. Water sparingly in winter ⬚ Leaf cuttings, leaves

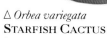

△ *Orbea variegata*
**STARFISH CACTUS**
↕ 10cm (4in) ↔ 30cm (12in)

Easy to grow and tolerant of neglect, this succulent forms clusters of toothed stems. The strong-smelling, star-shaped summer flowers have an exquisite mosaic pattern.

☼ Bright, with sun ◱ Warm, but cool to moderate in winter. Low humidity ◖ Monthly, using fertilizer for cacti and succulents ◊ When compost surface dry. Water sparingly in winter ⬚ Stem sections

△ *Lithops salicola*
**LIVING STONE**
↕ 5cm (2in) ↔ 23cm (9in)

One of a large group, from semi-desert regions of southern Africa, which mimic the pebbles among which they grow. It flowers from summer to mid-autumn.

☼ Bright, with sun ◱ Warm, but cool to moderate in winter. Low humidity ◖ Monthly, using fertilizer for cacti and succulents ◊ When compost surface dry. Water sparingly in winter ⬚ Offsets

△ *Mammillaria zeilmanniana* 'Ubinkii'
**ROSE PINCUSHION**
↕ 15cm (6in) ↔ 30cm (12in)

Excellent for beginners because it is free-flowering, even when young. Compact at first, then slowly dividing to form a broad cluster, it bears rose-pink spring flowers.

☼ Bright, with sun ◱ Warm, but cool to moderate in winter. Low humidity ◖ Monthly, using fertilizer for cacti and succulents ◊ When compost surface dry. Water sparingly in winter ⬚ Offsets

△ *Oreocereus trollii*
**OLD MAN OF THE ANDES**
↕ 90cm (3ft) ↔ 60cm (2ft)

This cactus, multi-branched when mature, forms erect, ribbed stems, clothed in long white hairs and lined with clusters of spines. Bears pink flowers in summer.

☼ Bright, with sun ◱ Warm, but cool to moderate in winter. Low humidity ◖ Monthly, using fertilizer for cacti and succulents ◊ When compost surface dry. Water sparingly in winter ⬚ Offsets

OTHER CACTI AND SUCCULENTS
FOR SPECIAL INTEREST

*Blossfeldia liliputana*
*Crassula falcata*
*Echinocactus grusonii*
*Echinocereus pectinatus*
*Euphorbia obesa*, see p.69
*Mammillaria hahniana*
*Opuntia verschaffeltii*
*Parodia leninghausii*, see p.61
*Rebutia spegazziniana*
*Sedum pachyphyllum*

△ *Pachyphytum oviferum*
## MOONSTONES
↕ 15cm (6in) ↔ 30cm (12in)

Clusters of smooth, egg-shaped, light green, white-bloomy leaves are flushed lavender-blue. Spikes of orange-red flowers are borne from winter to spring.

☼ Bright, with sun 🌡 Warm, but cool to moderate in winter. Low humidity 💧 Monthly, using fertilizer for cacti and succulents ⬤ When compost surface dry. Water sparingly in winter 🪴 Leaf cuttings

*Sedum morganianum* ▷
## BURRO'S TAIL, DONKEY'S TAIL
↕ 90cm (3ft) ↔ 30cm (12in)

This popular succulent, native to Mexico, has a prostrate habit in the wild but is usually grown in a hanging basket to show off its long, blue-green, leafy stems. ♈

☼ Bright, with sun 🌡 Warm, but cool to moderate in winter. Low humidity 💧 Monthly, using fertilizer for cacti and succulents ⬤ When compost surface dry. Water sparingly in winter 🪴 Stem cuttings

*Ribbed, spiny stem*

△ *Selenicereus grandiflorus*
## QUEEN OF THE NIGHT
↕ 3m (10ft) or more ↔ 1m (3ft) or more

A plant to enjoy at night – its 30cm (12in) long, richly fragrant, creamy-white flowers, borne in summer, open only after dark. The long stems need supporting.

☼ Bright, with sun 🌡 Warm, but moderate in winter. Low humidity 💧 Monthly, using fertilizer for cacti and succulents ⬤ When compost surface dry. Water sparingly in winter 🪴 Stem sections

*Pachypodium lamerei* ▷
## MADAGASCAR PALM
↕ 2m (6ft) or more
↔ 1.5m (5ft) or more

The spiny stems of this small, tree-like, eventually branching succulent bear long narrow leaves in terminal clusters. White, yellow-throated flowers appear in summer.

☼ Bright, with sun 🌡 Warm, but cool to moderate in winter. Low humidity 💧 Monthly, using fertilizer for cacti and succulents ⬤ When compost surface dry. Water sparingly in winter 🪴 Tip cuttings, seed

# Orchids for Special Interest

ORCHIDS ARE among the most coveted of all the flowering plant families, but contrary to popular belief they are not all the preserve of specialist growers; orchids are now available at many garden centres. Follow the cultivation notes given here, use a specialist orchid compost, and these plants will give endless satisfaction.

### *Cattleya* hybrids ▷
### CATTLEYA, CORSAGE ORCHID
↕ 20cm (8in) ↔ 45cm (18in)

Sumptuous and fragrant, these spring blooms are 12cm (5in) across and available in a range of colours. Grow in epiphytic orchid compost in a pot or orchid basket.

☼ Bright to moderate, avoiding direct sun ▯ Moderate to warm. High humidity ◍ Feed with every third watering ◌ When compost surface just moist. Water sparingly in winter ▤ Division

### △ *Miltoniopsis* hybrids
### PANSY ORCHID
↕ ↔ 23cm (9in)

These beautiful orchids produce large, fragrant, velvet-textured, pansy-like blooms in autumn. Grow in epiphytic orchid compost in a pot or orchid basket.

☼ Moderate to shady ▯ Moderate. High humidity ◍ Feed with every third watering ◌ When compost surface just dry. Reduce watering at lower temperatures ▤ Division

### *Cymbidium* hybrids ▷
### CYMBIDIUM
↕ 75cm (30in) ↔ 90cm (36in)

Among the most popular and reliable orchids for the home, with long-lasting flowers appearing from winter into spring. Available in a wide range of colours. Grow in any orchid compost.

☼ Bright, with some winter sun ▯ Moderate to warm. Moderate humidity ◍ Fortnightly, using half-strength flowering houseplant fertilizer. Monthly in winter ◌ Keep moist, but avoid waterlogging. Reduce watering in winter ▤ Division

### △ *Paphiopedilum insigne* hybrids
### SLIPPER ORCHID
↕ 15cm (6in) ↔ 25cm (10in)

Leathery basal leaves are complemented by leafless shoots, each bearing one or more large flowers with pouched lips from autumn until spring. Grow in a pot, using terrestrial orchid compost.

☼ Bright to moderate, avoiding direct sun ▯ Moderate to warm. High humidity ◍ Feed with every third watering. Occasionally in winter ◌ Keep moist. In winter, water when barely moist ▤ Division

---

OTHER ORCHIDS FOR SPECIAL INTEREST

x *Brassolaeliocattleya* hybrids
*Cattleya* mini hybrids
x *Doritaenopsis* hybrids
x *Laeliocattleya* hybrids
*Ludisia discolor*
*Phalaenopsis equestris* hybrids

---

*Widely arching, strap-shaped leaves*

*Phalaenopsis* hybrids ▷
**MOTH ORCHID**
↕ 1m (3ft) ↔ 45cm (18in)

Named the moth orchid after the wing-like shape of its blooms, which are borne in arching sprays throughout the year. Grow in epiphytic orchid compost in a basket or on a piece of bark.

☼ Bright, but avoid scorching sun
░ Warm, avoiding draughts. High humidity
◑ Fortnightly, using half-strength orchid fertilizer. Monthly in winter
◊ Keep moist, but avoid waterlogging
☷ Division

△ *Pleione bulbocodioides*
**PLEIONE**
↕ 15cm (6in) ↔ 5cm (2in)

A dwarf, spring-flowering orchid that likes cooler conditions than most, and is suited to a sunless windowsill. Grow in epiphytic orchid compost and allow a winter rest.

☼ Bright to moderate, avoiding direct sun ░ Cool to moderate. Moderate humidity ◑ Fortnightly when in leaf, using high potash fertilizer ◊ Keep moist after flowering. Keep dry when dormant ☷ Division

△ *Psychopsis papilio*
**BUTTERFLY ORCHID**
↕ 60cm (2ft) ↔ 30cm (12in)

This epiphytic orchid is a parent of several houseplant hybrids; its racemes of exquisite flowers are borne throughout the year. Grow in a basket or on bark.

☼ Moderate to shady, avoiding direct sun
░ Warm, avoiding fluctuation. High humidity
◑ Every three weeks ◊ Keep moist, but avoid waterlogging ☷ Division

---

**OTHER ORCHIDS FOR SPECIAL INTEREST**

*Colmanara* hybrids
*Cymbidium* mini hybrids
*Dendrodium nobile* (Yamamoto type) hybrids
*Dendrobium* × *Phalaenopsis* hybrids
× *Odontioda* hybrids
*Odontoglossum* hybrids
*Oncidium* hybrids
*Paphiopedilum primulinum* hybrids

---

*Ruffled flowers with marbled colour*

△ *Phragmipedium* hybrids
**SLIPPER ORCHID**
↕ ↔ 60cm (2ft)

These terrestrial orchids produce racemes of pouched flowers at intervals throughout the year. Best grown in epiphytic orchid compost in a pot that restricts the roots.

☼ Bright to moderate, avoiding direct sun
░ Moderate to warm. High humidity ◑ Feed with every third watering. Occasionally in winter ◊ Keep moist. In winter, water when just moist ☷ Division

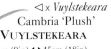

◁ × *Vuylstekeara*
Cambria 'Plush'
**VUYLSTEKEARA**
↕ 23cm (9in) ↔ 45cm (18in)

Ruffled, marbled flowers of many colours appear from spring to autumn on this popular plant, a hybrid of *Cochlioda*, *Miltonia*, and *Odontoglossum*. Grow it in epiphytic orchid compost.

☼ Bright to moderate, avoiding direct sun
░ Moderate to warm, but cool in winter. High humidity ◑ Monthly. Occasionally in winter
◊ Keep moist. Water sparingly in winter ☷ Division

# Palms for Special Interest

EW PLANTS bring a touch of the exotic to the home more readily than palms. Their often large, fan- or feather-shaped evergreen leaves provide any room with a focal point and a sense of visual drama. Palms grow in some of the world's wildest terrains, but many thrive indoors, where they will tolerate less than perfect conditions.

### *Caryota mitis* ▷
### BURMESE FISH-TAIL PALM
↕ 3m (10ft) or more ↔ 2m (6ft) or more

This plant is easily recognized by the characteristic fish-tail segments of its large, frond-like, arching leaves. A fairly easy palm to grow indoors, but it will need plenty of room in which to develop.

☼ Bright to moderate, avoiding summer sun
🌡 Moderate to warm. High humidity 💧 Fortnightly, using foliage houseplant fertilizer. Monthly in winter
💧 Water when dry. Avoid waterlogging 🌱 Seed

### *Chrysalidocarpus lutescens* ▷
### ARECA PALM
↕ 2m (6ft) or more ↔ 1.2m (4ft) or more

Naturally clump-forming, this popular palm from Madagascar has numerous erect, slender stems, initially clothed with yellow leaf bases. These later develop into arching, feathery, rich green leaves.

☼ Bright to moderate, avoiding hot sun 🌡 Moderate to warm. Moderate to high humidity 💧 Fortnightly, using foliage houseplant fertilizer. Monthly in winter
💧 Water when dry. Avoid waterlogging 🌱 Seed

### *Chamaedorea elegans* ▷
### PARLOUR PALM
↕ ↔ 2m (6ft)

Easily the most popular palm for the home, this plant is fast-growing, elegant, and tolerant of neglect and unfavourable conditions. It is found in Mexican rainforests.

☼ Bright to moderate. Avoid hot sun 🌡 Moderate to warm. Moderate to high humidity 💧 Fortnightly, using foliage houseplant fertilizer. Monthly in winter
💧 Water when dry. Avoid waterlogging 🌱 Seed

### *Cyrtostachys lakka* ▷
### SEALING-WAX PALM
↕ 3m (10ft) or more ↔ 1.5m (5ft) or more

One of the most beautiful and colourful palms, this native of south-east Asia has slender, brilliant scarlet stems supporting erect clusters of feathery leaves.

☼ Bright to moderate, avoiding summer sun
🌡 Warm. High humidity 💧 Fortnightly, using foliage houseplant fertilizer. Monthly in winter 💧 When compost surface dry. Avoid waterlogging 🌱 Seed

*Howea belmoreana* ▷
**SENTRY PALM**
↕ 3m (10ft) or more
↔ 2m (6ft) or more

A relative of the popular
kentia palm, *Howea
forsteriana*, and just as
tolerant of low light levels
and neglect. With maturity, the
leaves of the sentry palm develop their
large, curved, wide green leaflets.

☼ Bright to moderate, avoiding summer sun
❚▮ Warm. Moderate to high humidity ◐ Fortnightly,
using foliage houseplant fertilizer. Monthly in winter
◊ Water when dry. Avoid waterlogging ☷ Seed

*Phoenix roebelenii* ▷
**PYGMY DATE PALM**
↕ 3m (10ft) ↔ 2m (6ft) or more

With its spreading head of
feathery leaves, on a slender
stem rough with old leaf bases,
this is the perfect miniature
indoor palm tree. Tolerant of
low light levels and neglect, it
will thrive if given care. ♉

☼ Bright to moderate, avoiding
summer sun ❚▮ Moderate to warm.
Moderate to high humidity ◐ Fortnightly, using foliage houseplant
fertilizer. Monthly in winter ◊ Water
when dry. Avoid waterlogging ☷ Seed

**OTHER PALMS FOR SPECIAL
INTEREST**

*Caryota urens*
*Chamaedorea erumpens*
*Chamaedorea metallica*
*Chamaedorea stolonifera*
*Euterpe edulis*
*Hedyscepe canterburyana*
*Howea forsteriana*
  *Laccospadix australasica*
    *Lytocaryum weddellianum*, see p.97
    *Ravenea rivularis*, see p.73
    *Reinhardtia gracilis*

△ *Phoenix canariensis*
**CANARY ISLAND DATE PALM**
↕ 5m (15ft) or more ↔ 2m (6ft) or more

Large, pinnate leaves give this date palm
architectural interest. It is one of the most
common garden palms in warm regions of
the world, and a superb houseplant. ♉

☼ Bright to moderate. Avoid hot sun ❚▮ Moderate
to warm. Moderate humidity ◐ Fortnightly, using
foliage houseplant fertilizer. Monthly in winter
◊ Water when dry. Avoid waterlogging ☷ Seed

*Rhapis
excelsa* △
**LADY PALM**
↕ 3m (10ft) ↔ 1.2m (4ft)

A fine indoor palm with its dense clump
of erect, leafy, bamboo-like stems, the leaf
blades fan-shaped with long, fingered
segments. It is tolerant of neglect. ♉

☼ Bright to moderate. Avoid hot sun ❚▮ Moderate
to warm. Moderate humidity ◐ Fortnightly, using
foliage houseplant fertilizer. Monthly in winter
◊ Water when dry. Avoid waterlogging ☷ Seed

△ *Washingtonia robusta*
**SKYDUSTER**
↕ 3m (10ft) or more ↔ 2m (6ft)

Native to north-west Mexico, this fast-
growing palm enjoys good light and is
best suited to the garden room. Develops
a single stem with fan-shaped leaves.

☼ Bright to moderate. Avoid hot sun ❚▮ Moderate
to warm. Moderate humidity ◐ Fortnightly, using
foliage houseplant fertilizer. Monthly in winter
◊ Water when dry. Avoid waterlogging ☷ Seed

# Bromeliads for Special Interest

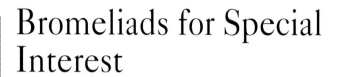

ALMOST ALL BROMELIADS originate in tropical or sub-tropical America. There is a multitude of species, varying remarkably in shape and colour, although most grown indoors are rosette-forming plants popular for foliage, flowers, or both. They look equally good in pots or hanging baskets.

△ *Billbergia* × *windii*
**BILLBERGIA**
↕ ↔ 60cm (2ft)

A handsome, clump-forming hybrid with long, arching, strap-shaped green leaves. It bears pendulous heads of green flowers from rose-pink bracts in summer.

☼ Bright, with some sun ▮ Moderate to warm. Moderate to high humidity ◗ Fortnightly, using flowering houseplant fertilizer ◌ Water when compost surface just dry ⊟ Offsets

△ *Aechmea morganii*
**URN PLANT**
↕ 60cm (2ft) ↔ 75cm (30in)

Striking for foliage and flowers, this big, bold bromeliad bears a rosette of glossy, dark green, strap-shaped, loosely arching leaves, and branched spikes of pink bracts and blue summer flowers.

☼ Bright, but avoid summer sun ▮ Warm. Low to moderate humidity ◗ Fortnightly, using flowering houseplant fertilizer ◌ Water when compost surface dry. Water sparingly in winter ⊟ Offsets

---

**OTHER BROMELIADS FOR FOLIAGE INTEREST**

*Ananas bracteatus* 'Tricolor', see p.60
*Billbergia* Fantasia Group
*Cryptanthus* 'Pink Starlight'
*Neoregelia carolinae* 'Tricolor Perfecta'
*Vriesea carinata*
*Vriesea* 'Tiffany'

---

◁ *Ananas comosus* 'Variegatus'
**IVORY PINEAPPLE**
↕ 90cm (3ft) ↔ 60cm (2ft)

Creamy-white-margined, dark green leaves, flushed red when young, make this pineapple special; the summer flowers, followed by the fruit, are a bonus. Place with care as the leaves are spiny.

☼ Bright ▮ Warm. Moderate to high humidity ◗ Fortnightly, using flowering houseplant fertilizer ◌ Water when compost surface just dry ⊟ Offsets, rosettes

△ *Cryptanthus zonatus* 'Zebrinus'
**EARTH STAR, ZEBRA PLANT**
↕ 12cm (5in) ↔ 40cm (16in)

A striking, star-shaped rosette plant with leathery, wavy-margined leaves, banded zebra fashion with dark grey-green and silver. Grows among rocks in east Brazil.

☼ Bright to shady, avoiding direct sun ▮ Warm. Moderate to high humidity ◗ Monthly, using flowering houseplant fertilizer. Rarely in winter ◌ Water when compost surface dry ⊟ Offsets

## △ *Neoregelia carolinae* f. *tricolor*
### BLUSHING BROMELIAD
↕ 30cm (12in) ↔ 60cm (2ft)

This spectacular Brazilian rainforest plant has a dense, bold rosette of spine-toothed, shiny green leaves, striped yellowish-white and red. In the summer flowering season, it has a red heart, hence its common name. ♔

☼ Bright, but avoid summer sun ◼ Warm. High humidity
◖ Fortnightly, using flowering houseplant fertilizer ◊ Water when compost surface dry ▤ Offsets

## *Tillandsia cyanea* ▷
### BLUE-FLOWERED TORCH
↕ 30cm (12in)
↔ 20cm (8in)

This striking epiphyte from Ecuador bears tufted rosettes of slender, curved and channelled leaves, topped in late spring or autumn by a paddle-shaped head of rose bracts and violet-blue flowers.

☼ Bright, but avoid direct sun ◼ Warm. Low to moderate humidity ◖ Every two months, using flowering houseplant fertilizer ◊ Water when compost surface dry ▤ Offsets

## △ *Vriesea hieroglyphica*
### KING OF BROMELIADS
↕ 90cm (3ft) ↔ 1m (39in)

An impressive plant, with purple-backed leaves that are yellowish-green with darker bands above. Yellow and green flowerheads are borne in summer on erect stems.

☼ Moderate ◼ Warm. Moderate to high humidity ◖ Every three weeks ◊ Water when compost surface dry ▤ Offsets, seed

---

### OTHER BROMELIADS FOR FLOWER AND BRACT INTEREST

*Aechmea chantinii*, see p.68
*Aechmea fasciata*, see p.26
*Aechmea* Foster's Favorite Group
*Billbergia nutans*
*Billbergia pyramidalis*
*Guzmania lingulata* var. *minor*
*Guzmania sanguinea*
*Tillandsia lindenii*

---

## ◁ *Tillandsia wagneriana*
### AIR PLANT
↕ ↔ 45cm (18in)

Unusual flower spikes with bracts of lavender adorn this epiphyte from the Peruvian Amazon in late spring or autumn, topping a bold, urn-shaped rosette of wavy-margined, crisp green or reddish leaves.

☼ Bright, but avoid direct sun ◼ Warm. Moderate to high humidity ◖ Every two months, using flowering houseplant fertilizer ◊ Water when compost surface dry ▤ Offsets

## △ *Vriesea splendens*
### FLAMING SWORD
↕ 90cm (3ft) ↔ 30cm (12in)

Worth growing for its rosettes of pale green leaves banded darker green, purple, or reddish brown. Red-scaled flowerheads on erect stems add summer interest. ♔

☼ Moderate, avoiding direct sun ◼ Moderate to warm. Moderate to high humidity ◖ Every three weeks, using flowering houseplant fertilizer ◊ Water when compost surface just dry ▤ Offsets

SPECIALIST PLANTS

117

# Novelty Houseplants

PLANTS THAT PROVIDE a talking point are welcome in any home. Spectacular flowers or impressive foliage always catch the eye, but so too do plants with an amusing growth habit or with some peculiarity of leaf or flower. Plants not usually grown indoors, or those with a fascinating history, also make good subjects. Novelty plants engage children's imaginations and with luck will inspire a desire to know more about plants.

△ *Dionaea muscipula*
**VENUS FLY TRAP**
↕ 45cm (18in) ↔ 15cm (6in)

A fascinating, carnivorous, short-lived perennial, of fierce appearance, that you can feed with flies or tiny fragments of raw meat. Prefers rain water to any other.

☀ Bright, with sun ▮ Moderate to warm. High humidity ♦ Feed if desired, but do not overfeed. Plant will also catch own food ◊ Stand pot in a tray and keep waterlogged ▦ Division, leaf cuttings

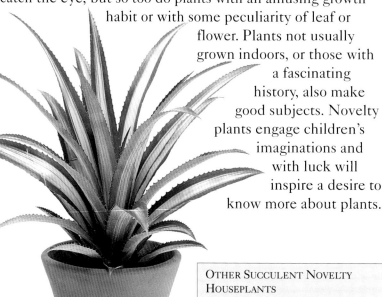

*Ananas comosus*
'Porteanus' △
**PINEAPPLE**
↕ 1m (3ft) ↔ 50cm (20in)

This plant has a handsome green and yellow rosette with spiny teeth. You can root a pineapple from the severed leafy top of a pineapple fruit, or try growing one from an offset.

☀ Bright, with sun ▮ Warm. Moderate to high humidity ♦ Fortnightly, using flowering houseplant fertilizer ◊ When just dry ▦ Offsets, rosettes

---

OTHER SUCCULENT NOVELTY HOUSEPLANTS

*Conophytum bilobum*
*Dorstenia foetida*
*Faucaria tigrina*, see p.57
*Fenestraria aurantiaca*
*Haworthia truncata*
*Kalanchoe daigremontiana*
*Lithops optica*
*Orbea variegata*, see p.110

---

*Capsicum annuum*
'Festival' ▷
**ORNAMENTAL PEPPER**
↕ ↔ 60cm (2ft)

Extremely ornamental and unusual, this small, bushy evergreen produces an eye-catching variety of different coloured fruits on one plant. It is normally treated as an annual and sold as an ornamental winter plant.

☀ Bright, but avoid direct sun ▮ Cool to moderate. Moderate humidity ♦ Fortnightly, alternating general fertilizer with flowering houseplant fertilizer ◊ When compost surface just dry ▦ Tip cuttings

△ *Epiphyllum laui*
**NIGHT-FLOWERING CACTUS**
↕ 30cm (12in) ↔ 60cm (2ft) or more

A night-flowering Mexican cactus whose fragrant, exotic-looking white flowers are produced in early summer (they may sometimes also open in daylight).

☀ Bright. Avoid direct sun ▮ Moderate to warm. Moderate to high humidity ♦ Fortnightly, from bud formation until flowering ends ◊ When just dry. Water sparingly in winter ▦ Stem cuttings, seed

*Euphorbia pulcherrima*
'Silver Star' ▷
**POINSETTIA**

↕ ↔ 50cm (20in)

Poinsettias seem to
be everywhere
in winter, but
this variety,
with its strange
mixture of leaf and
bract colours, is
uncommon. It
would make an
interesting addition to a group
of red-bracted poinsettias.

☀ Bright ▯ Warm, avoiding draughts and
fluctuating temperatures. Moderate to high
humidity ♦ Monthly ◊ Water when compost
surface just dry. Avoid waterlogging ▭ Tip cuttings

*Selaginella lepidophylla* ▷
**RESURRECTION PLANT**

↕ 8cm (3in) ↔ 15cm (6in)

Normally bought as a dried
ball (see inset), this plant will
uncurl into a rosette of rich green
ferny fronds when placed in a dish
of water or pot of damp compost.

☀ Shady ▯ Warm. High humidity ♦ Every five
weeks, using half-strength general houseplant fertilizer
◊ Water when compost surface just dry ▭ Stem cuttings

◁ *Mimosa pudica*
**SENSITIVE PLANT**

↕ 60cm (2ft) ↔ 40cm (16in)

Usually treated as an annual or
short-lived perennial, this fun plant
has ferny leaves that quickly fold
and droop when touched; be
careful not to overdo it as the plant
takes up to an hour to recover.

☀ Bright to moderate, avoiding direct sun
▯ Warm. High humidity ♦ Monthly
◊ When compost surface just dry. Reduce
watering in winter ▭ Seed

---

**OTHER NOVELTY HOUSEPLANTS**

*Arachis hypogaea*
*Darlingtonia californica*
*Davallia mariesii*
*Dracunculus vulgaris*
*Musa coccinea*
*Pinguicula grandiflora*
*Sarracenia flava*
*Tillandsia caput-medusae*, see p.57
*Tolmiea menziesii*, see p.67

*Olea europaea* ▷
**OLIVE**

↕ ↔ 3m (10ft) or more

A grey-leaved evergreen tree or bush,
easily kept small by pruning or training in
spring. Older plants produce tiny, fragrant
summer flowers that may bear fruit. ♈

☀ Bright, with sun ▯ Moderate to warm, but cool
in winter. Low humidity ♦ Monthly ◊ When
compost surface dry. Water sparingly in winter
▭ Semi-ripe cuttings, seed

△ *Streptocarpus wendlandii*
**CAPE PRIMROSE**

↕ 30cm (12in) ↔ 75cm (30in)

Very different to the usual Cape primrose,
this species has a single, enormous, dark
purple-green basal leaf, red-purple
beneath, and blue flowers in summer.

☀ Bright to moderate, avoiding direct sun
▯ Warm. Moderate to high humidity ♦ Fortnightly,
using flowering houseplant fertilizer ◊ When
compost surface just dry ▭ Seed

**SPECIALIST PLANTS**

# Index

Plants that are illustrated in the book are indicated by this symbol □

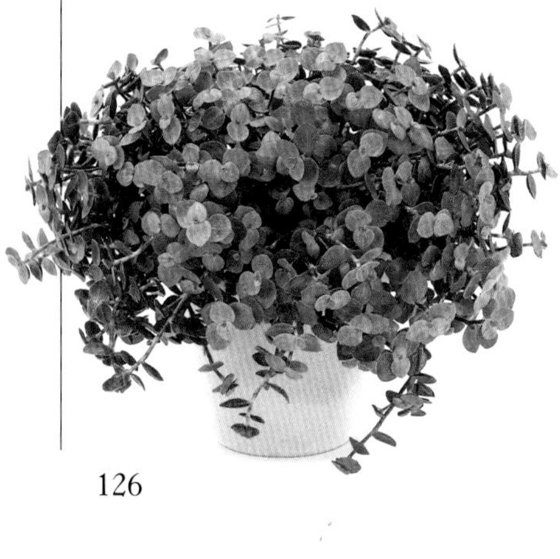

# Acknowledgments

**AUTHORS' ACKNOWLEDGMENTS:**
If we have learned anything in our pursuit of plant knowledge it is that who you know is often the basis of what you know, and this has certainly proved the case in the preparation of this book. Thus the ever-reliable Sarah Drew of the Hillier Plant Centre generously gave us the benefit of her "point of sales" experience, while Jim Gardiner, Curator of the RHS Garden, Wisley, and botanist Adrian Whiteley helped in their different ways. The following also gave us the benefit of their expertise: David Cooke, Royal Botanic Gardens, Kew; Dibley's Nurseries, Ruthin, North Wales; Maggie Garford, African Violet Centre, King's Lynn; John Gibson, Colegraves Seeds, Banbury; Alan Moon, Eric Young Orchid Foundation, Jersey; Stanley Mossop,

Boonwood Garden Centre, Cumbria; Dr. Henry Oakeley; and David Rhodes, Rhodes & Rockliffe, Essex. Thanks to our editor Clare Double and designer Helen Robson for their patience and understanding. We would also like to thank Sue Lancaster and Gill Biggs for their help, and Jessica Biggs for not interrupting.

**DORLING KINDERSLEY** would like to thank Martin Panter at Arnott and Mason, New Covent Garden, London, for plant supply and assistance with photography facilities; Matthew Ward for all his extra help; Lesley Riley for editorial assistance; Jane Parker for compiling the index; Antonia Johnson for proofreading; Charlotte Oster and Christine Rista for picture research; and Martin Hendry for design assistance.

**ILLUSTRATION CREDITS:**
Illustrations on pages 12–13 by Richard Lee.

**PHOTOGRAPHY CREDITS:**
Key: l=left, r=right, t=top, c=centre, b=bottom
Main photography by Matthew Ward, with additional photography by: Peter Anderson 15tl, 17tr, 19cl, 19bl, 20br, 92tl, 111tr, 111cr, 122; Deni Bown 47tl, 47bl, 89tc; Jonathan Buckley 33tl; Eric Crichton 112c, 113tc, 113bl; C. Andrew Henley 61bl, 81tc; Neil Fletcher 43br, 81tl; Dave King 2, 4, 16bl, 17cr, 22tr, 23, 37, 59, 85, 104tc, 107; Tom Dobbie 5cl, 24bl, 25tl, 25b, 26b, 27tr, 34br, 38br, 41t, 41bl, 41bc, 43tr, 44br, 46bl, 48c, 50tl,

51br, 52bc, 64bl, 66t, 67c, 67tr, 67c, 70br, 73bc, 75tl, 75br, 78b, 79tl, 82tr, 82br, 83br, 86b, 87tl, 87c, 87b, 88b, 90bl, 92c, 92 tr, 93bl, 93tr, 94tl, 94bl, 95tr, 95br, 97bc, 98bl, 100tl, 101tl, 102tr, 102br, 103tc, 103br, 108bl, 109tl, 109c, 109b, 114bl, 115tl, 115br; John Fielding 81cl; Andrew Lawson 60br; Andrew de Lory 51br; Howard Rice 27c, 46tr, 63br, 66bl, 87tr, 100bl, 103tl; Bob Rundle 94br; Juliette Wade 31tr; Steven Wooster 33tc, 103tr. Other Dorling Kindersley photographs by Peter Anderson, Eric Crichton, Christine Douglas, John Fielding, Neil Fletcher, John Glover, Jerry Harpur, Sunniva Harte, C. Andrew Henley, Andrew Lawson, Andrew de Lory, Jacqui Hurst, Howard Rice, Bob Rundle, Juliette Wade, David Watts, and Steven Wooster.

Dorling Kindersley is grateful to the following for permission to reproduce photographs: Gillian Beckett 31tl, 74t; Matthew Biggs 68tl; Bruce Coleman Collection / Jules Cowan 11tl; Dibley's Nurseries, North Wales 35br; The Garden Picture Library / Lynne Brotchie 9b / Howard Rice 36tr / Friedrich Strauss 8bl, 22cr, 84br, 106tr / Michel Viard 106b / Steven Wooster 58bl; Harpur Garden Library 8t, 22bl, 36bl; Houses and Interiors / Simon Butcher 12tl /Fotodienst Fehn 84bl; International Interiors / Paul Ryan 13tr, 13bl; Roy Lancaster 11br, 30br, 31tc, 42tl, 80br, 80tr; Photos Horticultural 51tc; Planet Earth Pictures / Robert Jureit 10b; View / Dennis Gilbert 9t; Elizabeth Whiting Associates / Graham Henderson 12br / Spike Powell 58t.